T0319752

Modelling Tax Revenue Growth

Modelling Tax Revenue Growth

John Creedy
Truby Williams Professor of Economics,
University of Melbourne, Australia

Norman Gemmell
Professorial Research Fellow, School of Economics,
University of Nottingham, UK

Edward Elgar
Cheltenham, UK • Northampton, MA, USA

Published by
Edward Elgar Publishing Limited
Glensanda House
Montpellier Parade
Cheltenham
Glos GL50 1UA
UK

Edward Elgar Publishing, Inc.
136 West Street
Suite 202
Northampton
Massachusetts 01060
USA

A catalogue record for this book
is available from the British Library

Library of Congress Cataloguing in Publication Data
Creedy, John, 1949-
  Modelling tax revenue growth / John Creedy, Norman Gemmell.
    p. cm.
  Includes bibliographical references and index.
  ISBN 1-84542-703-3
  1. Tax revenue estimating. 2. Taxation. 3. Elasticity (Economics) I.
Gemmell, Norman. II. Title.

HJ2351.4.C74 2006
336.2001'12—dc22   2005054312

ISBN-13: 978 1 84542 703 X
ISBN-10: 1 84542 703 3

Printed and bound in Great Britain by MPG Books Ltd, Bodmin, Cornwall

Contents

Figures

Tables

Acknowledgements

Some of the chapters in this book are based on journal publications by the authors, though in each case the material has been substantially revised and rearranged. We are grateful to the publishers of those journals for permission to use the material here, and to the numerous referees who provided constructive comments. The journal publications include Creedy and Gemmell (2002a, 2002b, 2003, 2004a, 2004b, 2005).

Part I

Introduction

Chapter 1

Introduction

1.1 Key Concepts and Measures

Measuring the long–run growth of tax revenues reliably, both for a tax system and for its component taxes, is important for the design of tax policy. When fiscal authorities set some revenue target, for example, the need for discretionary changes in tax parameters (such as tax rates, income thresholds and allowances) is conditional on the expected automatic revenue growth generated by the tax system in the absence of any discretionary change. The properties which generate these automatic revenue changes are referred to as the built–in flexibility, or revenue responsiveness, of the tax. A commonly used, unit–free measure of this responsiveness is the revenue elasticity of the tax. This is the percentage change in tax revenue in response to a given percentage change in income, for a constant tax structure.

These concepts are the central focus of the analyses in this book. The purpose of the book is to provide a review and synthesis of analytical results on the key concept of tax revenue elasticity, and to demonstrate how this concept can be applied in practice to yield estimates of revenue responsiveness in various countries. In general, the elasticity expressions derived below are both tractable and readily applied to the kinds of summary tax data that are available for most tax systems.

Revenue elasticity is a useful summary measure of built–in flexibility for a number of reasons. Firstly, to identify discretionary effects on tax revenues, the revenue elasticity may be compared with tax buoyancy. This is the total change in tax revenue observed in association with changes in income. Thus, for example, a buoyancy value of 1.5 indicates that observed revenue increased 50 per cent faster than income increased (over a given period). A comparable revenue elasticity of 1.3 would imply that, with an unchanged tax structure, revenues would have risen 30 per cent faster than incomes. Secondly, tax elasticity is closely related to tax progressivity – the redistributional properties of a tax – so tax changes designed to affect progressivity may have unintended consequences for elasticity, and *vice versa*: on progressivity and elasticity, see Podder (1997).

Thirdly, estimates of tax revenue elasticities can assist in long–run revenue forecasting. Such forecasts are often conditional on income growth projections, for a constant tax structure. Fourthly, the built–in flexibility of taxation is known to affect the stability properties of macroeconomic models. The large literature on this issue includes Smyth (1974, 1978), Delorme and Hayakawa (1977), Özmucur (1979), Peel (1979), and Pohjola (1985). An elastic tax acts as an automatic stabiliser: when the economy is in recession and incomes are falling (or rising slowly), tax revenues fall proportionately more (or rise more slowly) so helping to maintain the growth of disposable incomes or spending. Understanding the principle determinants of a tax system's revenue responsiveness, and a knowledge of the relevant magnitudes, are therefore important for the design and reform of tax policy, where both revenue and redistributional considerations are typically central to the policy agenda.

This book examines tax revenue elasticity in the context of personal income and consumption taxes. Consumption or indirect taxes here refer to taxes levied directly on goods rather than on individuals; hence individuals are taxed indirectly. This book provides a unifying framework within which analytical expressions for the revenue elasticities of various taxes may be compared and combined. This is the main focus of Part II. Early studies based on analytical expressions for income tax revenue elasticities include Hutton and Lambert (1980, 1982a) and Creedy and Gemmell (1984, 1985) for the UK; and Friedlaender *et al.* (1973), Fries *et al.* (1982) and Fox and Campbell (1984) for the US. Dorrington (1974), Spahn (1975) and Hutton and Lambert (1982b) used simulation methods to examine the elasticity of income taxation.

Part II also demonstrates that these elasticity expressions can readily be used to estimate revenue responsiveness in practice and, in most cases, estimates of the relevant elasticities require information on a relatively small number of parameters. Using readily available data, Part III examines three case studies, estimating the revenue responsiveness of income and consumption taxes in the UK, Australia and New Zealand. The tax systems of these three countries, with their shared historical influences, retain many similarities, but have also evolved in quite different ways in recent decades. However, the key built–in flexibility properties which they share are also common to many other countries' income and consumption tax systems. The methods used here should therefore have a much wider applicability.

The approach described in this book, involving explicit modelling of the tax structure, contrasts with the common empirical approach involving simulation models or regression analyses of time–series data on tax revenues and income, which are sometimes used to produce aggregate elasticities. For example, the UK revenue forecasting models employed by the UK Treasury and the Institute for Fiscal Studies (IFS) either estimate or impose tax revenue elasticities. These attempt to capture the relationship between the tax revenue yield and a measure of the tax base such as income, for given tax rates. The UK Treasury and IFS revenue forecasting methods are discussed in Pike and Savage (1998) and Giles and Hall (1998) respectively.

Attempts to measure tax elasticities relying on regression methods applied to data on various tax revenue, tax base and income aggregates, have a long history. These include Vickrey (1949), Groves and Kahn (1952), Smith (1963), Wilford (1965), Legler and Shapiro (1968), Tanzi (1969, 1976), Singer (1970), Friedlaender *et al.* (1973), Wasylenko (1975), Suyderhoud and Veseth (1976), Greytak and Thursby (1979), Carter (1981), Fox and Campbell (1984), Dye and McGuire (1991), Ram (1991), Sobel and Holcombe (1996). For a number of Organisation for Economic Cooperation and Development (OECD) countries, van den Noord (2000) and Heinemann (2001) used regression methods to estimate various tax revenue elasticities for personal income and indirect taxes, with respect to changes in GDP or other income measures. Also Giorno *et al.* (1995) provided some comparisons of aggregate income tax revenue elasticities based both on regressions and on tax–share weighted individual values for OECD countries.

These empirical methods are typically applied to fairly aggregate–level data and, because they do not model changes in the tax structure formally or precisely, often struggle to measure tax elasticity, as distinct from tax buoyancy. An alternative numerical approach is to model the tax structure explicitly and apply it to a large taxpayer micro dataset. When it is desired to produce detailed short–run revenue forecasts, or projections for particular groups or types of taxpayer, this approach may be the most accurate. However it is usually only available to official forecasters with access to detailed taxpayer records. In addition, it is generally unable to separate the impacts of the various determinants of revenue elasticities. These alternative methods are not explored in this book.

A common feature of all these approaches to measuring revenue responsiveness, whether based on regression or simulation methods, or calculations using analytical expressions, is that they are essentially statistical in nature. That is, there is no modelling of economic behaviour, with income changes treated as exogenous, so that no allowance is made for endogenous labour supply effects on revenue elasticities. This may partly reflect the perception that labour supply effects are sufficiently small, in terms of their effects on aggregate tax revenues, that they can be ignored. In addition, it is likely to be difficult to introduce such endogeneity into regression methods. However, chapter 4 below shows how labour supply effects may be integrated into the revenue responsiveness expressions for income taxes, and identifies a number of variables on which the quantitative importance of these effects depends.

The issue of revenue responsiveness is most often thought of in relation to fiscal drag, the phenomenon whereby growth in nominal incomes, with a fixed tax structure, shifts individuals into higher income tax brackets causing income tax revenues to grow faster than incomes. In principle, indexation of tax thresholds to prices can eliminate this, though the form of price indexation can be important. However, fiscal drag associated with an income tax has implications for consumption tax revenues which are often not appreciated. Also, with a tendency for real incomes to grow over time, but with thresholds indexed to prices, real fiscal drag remains a relevant issue for revenue projections. However, a focus on either of these fiscal drag effects can be misleading. As the empirical analysis in chapter 5 demonstrates for the UK, the major influences on revenue elasticities in practice are often the discretionary changes in fiscal parameters by the budgetary authorities, and endogenous responses by taxpayers to new or reformed tax regimes, rather than the more commonly recognised effects of fiscal drag.

1.2   A Non–technical Summary

The analysis of revenue responsiveness in Part II of this book takes the form of algebraic expressions for revenue elasticities which are then applied to data in Part III. These expressions, and their derivations, can appear complex but in essence capture simple processes for which the intuition is relatively straightforward. For both income and consumption taxes, the primary interest is in the percentage change in tax revenues in response to a given percentage change in income, for a constant tax structure – the revenue elasticity of the tax. This can be examined both for individual taxpayers and for taxpayers in aggregate. In the case of the latter, information is required on the distribution of income across individuals as well as the relevant tax parameters.

In the case of personal income taxes, gross earned income is the base on which the tax is typically levied directly. Changes in gross income therefore can be expected to have an immediate, direct effect on income tax payments. Consumption taxes include *ad valorem* taxes such as Value Added Tax (VAT) and excises levied as a fixed monetary amount per unit, rather than as a percentage of the unit price, on such items as tobacco, alcohol or motor fuel. For these taxes, the direct tax base is expenditure, or tax–liable expenditure (for example, spending on cigarettes). Estimating the impact of changes in gross income on revenues is therefore less straightforward for consumption taxes. This involves several responses to changes in gross incomes, including changes in disposable income affected by income tax changes, changes in total expenditures if saving behaviour changes, and changes to tax–liable expenditure if, for example, consumption patterns change towards or away from taxed goods. Only after these responses have been modelled or estimated can information on consumption tax structures be applied to generate the automatic change in consumption tax revenues arising from the initial change in income.

Table 1.1 summarises the main components in the derivation of consumption tax revenue elasticities, and introduces the key terminology used throughout this book. The example illustrates the case of an individual facing an income tax with a single tax rate, and an *ad valorem* indirect tax levied on specified expenditures at a single rate. Because income tax paid is one determinant of available expenditures, the example also serves to illustrate the contributors to the consumption tax elasticity.

Row 5 of Table 1.1 shows the income tax calculation for this simple case.

Table 1.1: The Consumption Tax Calculation

No.		Category	Symbol	Comment
1.		Income	y	
2.	*minus*	Allowances	a	a = allowance against
3.	=	Taxable income	$(y-a)$	income tax
4.	*times*	Tax rate	t	
5.	=	**Income tax**	T_y	$T_y = t(y-a)$
6.	*1 – 5 =*	Disposable income	z	$z = y - T_y$
7.	*minus*	Savings	$(1-\gamma)z$	γ = prop. of z spent
8.	=	Total expenditure	m	$m = \gamma(y - T_y)$
9.	*minus*	Untaxed expenditure	$(1-w_\ell)m$	w_ℓ = prop. of m
				liable to cons. tax
10.	=	Taxable expenditure	m_ℓ	$m_\ell = w_\ell\gamma(y - T_y)$
11.	*times*	Consumption tax rate	$\frac{v_\ell}{1+v_\ell}$	v_ℓ = tax rate on tax-
				exclusive price
12.	=	**Consumption tax**	T_{v_ℓ}	$= \frac{v_\ell}{1+v_\ell}m_\ell$
				$= \frac{v_\ell}{1+v_\ell}w_\ell\gamma(y - T_y)$

This depends on three elements: the income tax rate, income and allowances against income. In this simple case, if both tax parameters (t and a) are fixed, changes in tax revenues could only reflect any changes in income. However, as chapter 2 shows, even when there are no discretionary changes to tax parameters, these may be related to income and so change endogenously when income changes. Also, in more complex multi–step tax structures, movements across tax thresholds (including into and out of taxpayer status) can affect revenue elasticity calculations. This serves to highlight an important aspect of revenue responsiveness. Although revenue elasticities measure revenue responses for a given tax structure, the tax structure can affect the value of revenue elasticities. Hence, different structures for the same tax have different built–in flexibility properties. As a result a change in tax structure has two effects – an immediate direct effect on revenue levels, and an indirect, or automatic, effect on future revenue growth via changes to the revenue elasticity.

The main terminology and derivation of the consumption tax liability calculations are also introduced in Table 1.1. This culminates, in row 12, with the key parameters and variables shown in the right–hand column. In non–algebraic terms this can be written as:

$$
\begin{Bmatrix} \text{Tax paid} \\ \text{on} \\ \text{good } \ell \end{Bmatrix} = \begin{Bmatrix} \text{tax} \\ \text{rate} \\ \text{on } \ell \end{Bmatrix} \begin{Bmatrix} \text{budget} \\ \text{share of} \\ \text{good } \ell \end{Bmatrix} \begin{Bmatrix} \text{prop of} \\ \text{net inc.} \\ \text{spent} \end{Bmatrix} \begin{Bmatrix} \text{income} \\ -\text{ inc. tax} \\ +\text{ transfers} \end{Bmatrix}
$$

Consumption tax revenue is determined in this simple case, firstly by the individual's income, less any income tax payments made, T_y, plus any transfer payments received, for example social security payments. This determines income available for spending, but the proportion of after–income–tax (disposable) income that is spent, γ, the proportion of that spending on the tax–liable good, w_ℓ, and the tax rate on this good, v_ℓ, each subsequently affect consumption tax payments. The value of, and changes in, each of these components as income changes can affect the revenue elasticity of consumption taxes. To understand the influences on this elasticity it is therefore important to know about the progressivity of the income tax system, individuals' savings habits (how these change with income), any shifts in consumption preferences when incomes change, and the structure of indirect tax rates.

Chapter 3 shows that the simplicity or complexity of the resulting revenue elasticity expressions is influenced by the structure of both income and consumption taxes. As might be expected, tax systems with multiple taxes and several tax rates yield more complex expressions for both individual and overall revenue elasticities. However, in all cases the elasticity of a tax can be expressed as:

$$
\text{Revenue elasticity} = \frac{\text{Marginal tax rate}}{\text{Average tax rate}}
$$

The revenue elasticity is thus readily calculated once both average and marginal tax rates are known. As the analysis in later chapters demonstrates, this is not always as straightforward as it may appear. In particular, the effective marginal tax rate faced by an individual may be quite different from the statutory or legal rate, with knock–on effects for the average tax rate. This divergence between effective and statutory rates arises primarily where taxpayers can off–set various allowances and deductions against tax.

The description above relates to the revenue elasticities for an individual taxpayer. These are of interest in part because they can help to identify the impact on the growth of tax liabilities for different individuals facing different circumstances, or for the same individual over time. However, for tax policy purposes, it is often the aggregate elasticity for all taxpayers that is of most concern. To measure this requires information of the income distribution and how individual incomes within it, change over time. As subsequent chapters show, where it can be assumed that all incomes grow in equal proportion over time, aggregate revenue elasticity expressions are more easily specified. However, in practice this equiproportionate case is rarely observed, so that allowing for changes in the income distribution can be important for elasticity measurement.

1.3   Outline of Future Chapters

This section summarises the analysis and results from the three chapters in Part II which deal with conceptual issues (chapters 2–4) and the three chapters in Part III applying these in the UK, Australian and New Zealand contexts (chapters 5–7). Some conclusions are drawn together in chapter 8.

1.3.1   Conceptual Issues

Chapter 2 concentrates on the revenue elasticity of income taxes, and provides a unified framework in which to examine analytical elasticity expressions. The analytical results synthesised and extended here help to provide both an understanding of the determinants of the revenue responsiveness

properties of different income tax structures, and convenient expressions for
the calculation of elasticities in practice. It shows that the magnitude of revenue elasticities can be expected to differ substantially for alternative forms
of income tax, and for the same tax over time as, for example, incomes change
relative to tax thresholds.

The various parameters in the tax elasticity expressions highlight a number of potential impacts of tax reform on revenue elasticities. For example,
tax reforms are often undertaken to achieve particular revenue and/or redistributive objectives in the short–to–medium run, or to be revenue–neutral or
distribution–neutral. It is, however, less well appreciated that changes in tax
progressivity often imply changes in elasticities, while (short–run) revenue–
neutral changes are not necessarily 'elasticity–neutral'.

Chapter 3 shows that tractable analytical expressions can be produced
for the revenue elasticities of various indirect taxes and for combined direct–
plus–indirect taxes, where the indirect tax system is combined with a general
multi–step income tax structure. These results clarify the determinants of
the revenue responsiveness properties of indirect taxes, and demonstrate that
revenue elasticities for such taxes can be estimated from information that is
generally available for most tax systems: summary tax parameters and total
expenditure elasticities for commodity groups.

Two simple, but useful, results are demonstrated in this chapter. First,
in a uniform consumption tax rate system, consumption tax revenue must
be income–inelastic provided the income tax system is progressive. The elasticity of total income–plus–consumption taxes, however, must exceed unity.
Second, for the more common two–rate or multi–rate cases, whether or not
consumption tax revenue is elastic is ambiguous, and depends on the progressivity of the income tax and the (average) expenditure elasticity of taxed
goods. Consumption taxes are less likely to be elastic if income taxes are
progressive, but more likely to be elastic if tax–exempt goods are mainly
necessities.

Chapter 4 extends the analysis of chapter 2 for income taxes to accommodate the endogenous response of labour supply to the income tax system. It shows how revenue elasticity expressions can be adapted to allow for growth in wage rates which, together with endogenous labour supply responses, determines income growth. Over the long run it is probably more appropriate to treat the growth of wage rates, rather than incomes, as determined by exogenous productivity growth. The primary objective of this chapter is to identify how far, and in what circumstances, labour supply effects are quantitatively important for revenue responsiveness estimates, both for individual taxpayers and in aggregate.

Analytical elasticity expressions derived in chapter 4 show the importance of income tax rates and thresholds, the elasticity of income tax allowances with respect to wages, and the labour supply elasticity. The last of these is a function of the wage and tax structures and leisure preferences. To quantify these various determinants, a numerical exercise is used based on a stylised version of the UK income tax and transfer system. For individuals (especially those on low wages where income taxes and transfers interact, and those close to income tax thresholds), this shows that even a relatively simple tax–benefit structure can produce labour supply responses which considerably alter tax revenue elasticity calculations.

Results in aggregate suggest that tax–income elasticities may provide a reasonable approximation of tax–wage responses but only in the presence of a relatively strong preference for consumption over leisure. However, for particular groups of individuals (such as women, pension recipients, and low–wage men) tax revenue elasticities may need to allow for labour supply responses.

1.3.2 Applications

Having derived conceptual elasticity expressions for a variety of taxes, chapter 5 applies these to the revenue responsiveness properties of UK income and consumption taxes, from the late 1980s onwards. The results reveal that an important component of the revenue elasticity – the income elasticity of income–related deductions – appears to be variable over time. It fell substantially with the limitation, and then withdrawal, of mortgage interest tax relief in the early 1990s, but has risen again in recent years with the rise in private pension schemes. Income tax revenue elasticities also appear to have been rising during the 1990s, from around 1.2 in 1990 to 1.4 by 2000, partly in response to the increased deductions referred to above, and the reversal of some of the 1980s tax reforms which had previously flattened the income tax structure.

Elasticities for consumption taxes are often presumed to be close to unity, and this appears to be confirmed when consumers' savings and transfer payments are ignored. However, when the impacts of savings behaviour, transfers and changing consumption patterns towards tax–liable goods are recognised, values for the revenue elasticity as low as 0.7 are obtained for recent years. With consumption tax buoyancy around 1.4 over this period, discretionary tax changes would appear to have substantially raised revenues in this case.

Revenue elasticity and tax progressivity are closely related concepts. Chapter 6 examines the extent to which redistribution can be achieved using only a structure of consumption taxes with differential rates and exemptions, taking the Australian case as an example. Although redistribution can be achieved by taxing most heavily those goods for which the income (expenditure) elasticity exceeds unity (for which the budget shares increase as income increases), there are strong limitations. This arises from the fact that virtually all households consume some goods in each commodity group (given a broad classification) and expenditure elasticities ultimately tend to unity as income rises.

The issue is examined by considering a local measure of progression – that of liability progression – which is equivalent to the revenue elasticity with respect to total expenditure. Progressivity is found to be maximised when only one commodity group, that having the largest total expenditure elasticity, is taxed. Where further commodity groups need to be taxed to meet revenue requirements, the tax rate should fall as the total expenditure elasticity falls. With a uniform structure, but where some goods are exempt from the consumption tax, liability progression is shown to be independent of the level of the tax rate. Chapter 6 then examines the actual Australian indirect tax structure along with a hypothetical alternative where only luxuries are taxed. It is found that even extreme forms of differentiation in indirect taxes have a relatively small effect on liability progression and inequality. The results confirm the common suggestion that consumption taxes provide, at most, a blunt redistributive instrument.

Chapter 7 examines the revenue responsiveness properties of New Zealand income and consumption taxes, based on the 2001 tax structure and expenditure patterns. Using the analytical expressions derived in earlier chapters, revenue elasticity estimates are reported for a range of income levels. Treating income growth as equiproportionate, these suggest that the aggregate income and consumption tax revenue elasticities are both fairly constant as mean income increases, at around 1.3 and 1.0 respectively. Allowing for non–equiproportionate income growth reduces revenue elasticities to around 1.1 for income tax and 0.93 for consumption taxes. If there is a tendency for the savings proportion to increase as disposable income increases, a somewhat lower total consumption tax revenue elasticity, of around 0.85–0.90, is obtained at mean incomes approximating current levels in New Zealand. Further it would seem that, despite the adoption of a broad based goods and services tax (GST) at a uniform rate in New Zealand, the persistence of various excises has an important effect on the overall consumption tax revenue elasticity, especially for individuals at relatively low income levels. This is confirmed by revenue elasticity estimates for individual excises such as those levied on vehicles, fuel, alcohol and tobacco.

Part II

Concepts

Chapter 2

Income Tax Revenue Elasticities

This chapter provides a review and synthesis of analytical results on the revenue responsiveness or 'built–in flexibility' of income tax, measured by the elasticity of tax revenue with respect to income. It is shown that in most cases estimates of the relevant elasticities require information on a relatively small number of parameters.

Section 2.1 begins with basic tax elasticity definitions for the individual taxpayer. The associated aggregate revenue elasticities are the focus of section 2.2. Section 2.3 derives elasticity expressions for the most commonly used income tax function, the multi–step case. Several nonlinear tax functions are examined in section 2.5, and the computation of aggregate elasticities is discussed in section 2.6. Conclusions are in section 2.7.

2.1 Individual Revenue Elasticities

This section is concerned with revenue elasticities at the individual level. Suppose $T(y_i)$ denotes the income tax paid by individual i with a nominal income of y_i. Throughout this chapter all references to income variables relate to nominal values. Thus changes in nominal income with respect to nominal tax allowances affect built–in flexibility, except for the case (discussed below) where the tax function is homogeneous of degree one in income and allowances, and both are indexed in the same way to prices.

The individual revenue elasticity of the income tax with respect to a change in income, η_{T_y, y_i}, is defined, following the conventional elasticity concept, as the proportional change in tax divided by the proportional change in the individual's income. Hence:

$$\eta_{T_y, y_i} = \frac{dT(y_i)/T(y_i)}{dy_i/y_i} \tag{2.1}$$

so that a simple rearrangement gives:

$$\eta_{T_y, y_i} = \frac{dT(y_i)/dy_i}{T(y_i)/y_i} = \frac{mtr_i}{atr_i} \tag{2.2}$$

where mtr_i is the marginal tax rate and atr_i is the average tax rate faced by i. The general scheme adopted here for notation is that the first subscript of the revenue elasticity, η, refers to the type of tax revenue considered and the second subscript refers to the income that is considered to change. However, in the present case of the individual elasticity, the first subscript T_y is used as a shorthand for $T(y_i)$. In a progressive tax structure, $mtr_i > atr_i$ for all i, so that $\eta_{T_y, y_i} > 1$. This elasticity is also the local measure of liability progression defined by Musgrave and Thin (1948).

Further insight into the revenue elasticity can be obtained by considering the variation in the average tax rate as income increases.

$$\frac{d}{dy_i}\left(\frac{T(y_i)}{y_i}\right) = \frac{1}{y_i}\left[\frac{dT(y_i)}{dy_i} - \frac{T(y_i)}{y_i}\right] \tag{2.3}$$

This is Musgrave and Thin's measure of average rate progression. The term in square brackets in (2.3) is the difference between the marginal and average tax rates, which is positive for a progressive tax. The elasticity of the average tax rate with respect to income, η_{atr, y_i}, is given by:

$$
\begin{aligned}
\eta_{atr, y_i} &= \left(\frac{y_i}{T(y_i)/y_i}\right)\frac{d}{dy_i}\left(\frac{T(y_i)}{y_i}\right) \\
&= \frac{1}{T(y_i)/y_i}\left[\frac{dT(y_i)}{dy_i} - \frac{T(y_i)}{y_i}\right] \\
&= \eta_{T_y, y_i} - 1 \tag{2.4}
\end{aligned}
$$

Hence the revenue elasticity can be expressed as:

$$\eta_{T_y, y_i} = 1 + \eta_{atr, y_i} \tag{2.5}$$

This result shows that an increase in η_{atr, y_i}, that is a higher rate of increase in the average tax rate at the income y_i, results in a higher revenue elasticity at y_i. Hence η_{atr, y_i} can change even though mtr_i is fixed if, for example, allowances change. Furthermore, from (2.4) a progressive tax, for which $\eta_{atr, y_i} > 0$, is necessarily an elastic tax. Measuring this elasticity only requires information about average tax rates at different income levels which is often readily available. In the UK for example, the Inland Revenue publishes annual estimates of average income tax rates at a variety of income levels. This allows elasticity estimates to be obtained even without detailed knowledge of the tax function.

2.2 The Aggregate Revenue Elasticity

For tax policy purposes the aggregate, rather than the individual, tax revenue elasticity is often more relevant. In this context the form of the distribution of income becomes important. Nevertheless a number of the results from the previous section carry over to the case of many individuals in a straightforward way.

Suppose there are N individuals, with incomes $y_1, ..., y_N$, so that total income, Y, is $\sum_{i=1}^{N} y_i$, and total income tax revenue, T_Y, is $\sum_{i=1}^{N} T(y_i)$. Totally differentiating aggregate revenue gives:

$$dT_Y = \sum_{i=1}^{N} \frac{\partial T(y_i)}{\partial y_i} dy_i \tag{2.6}$$

so that the aggregate elasticity is:

$$
\frac{dT_Y}{T_Y}\frac{Y}{dY} = \sum_{i=1}^{N} \left\{ \frac{\partial T(y_i)}{T(y_i)}\frac{y_i}{\partial y_i} \right\} \left\{ \frac{dy_i}{y_i}\frac{Y}{dY} \right\} \left\{ \frac{T(y_i)}{T_Y} \right\}
$$

$$
= \sum_{i=1}^{N} \left(\eta_{T_y,y_i} \right) \left(\eta_{y_i,Y} \right) \left\{ \frac{T(y_i)}{T_Y} \right\} \tag{2.7}
$$

Therefore the elasticity of aggregate revenue with respect to a change in aggregate income, $\eta_{T_Y,Y}$, is a tax–share weighted average of the product of individual revenue elasticities, η_{T_y,y_i}, and the elasticity of individual income with respect to total income, $\eta_{y_i,Y}$, with $\sum_{i=1}^{N} \eta_{y_i,Y} = 1$. This means that the aggregate elasticity cannot be obtained without specifying the distribution of proportionate income changes, dy_i/y_i, associated with any proportional increase in total income, dY/Y. For non–equiproportional changes, the aggregate revenue elasticity can be less than 1; for example it is zero if the only incomes which increase are below a tax–free threshold and none crosses the threshold.

2.2.1 Equiproportional Income Changes

The simplest form of (2.7) is for the special case where all individuals experience an equal proportionate increase in income. Any relative measure of inequality is unchanged and $dy_i/y_i = dY/Y$, so that $\eta_{y_i,Y} = 1$ for all i. Substituting into (2.7) gives:

$$
\eta_{T_Y,Y} = \sum_{i=1}^{N} \eta_{T_y,y_i} \frac{T(y_i)}{T_Y} \tag{2.8}
$$

Hence, the aggregate elasticity is in this case simply a weighted average of the individual elasticities, with weights equal to the proportion of total revenue paid by each individual. The majority of empirical analyses have used this simplifying assumption.

   With equiproportional income changes, further insight can be obtained using the approach of Lambert (1993, pp. 155–156). Suppose that all incomes increase from y_i to θy_i. Writing the aggregate tax function as $T_Y(Y)$, the new revenue is given by:

$$T_Y(\theta Y) = \sum_{i=1}^{N} T(\theta y_i) \qquad (2.9)$$

Differentiating with respect to θ and setting $\theta = 1$ it can be shown that the aggregate effective marginal tax rate, MTR, is an income–share weighted average of the individual marginal tax rates. Hence:

$$T_Y'(Y) = \sum_{i=1}^{N} \left(\frac{y_i}{Y}\right) T'(y_i) \qquad (2.10)$$

and:

$$\eta_{T_Y,Y} = \frac{\sum_{i=1}^{N} y_i T'(y_i)}{\sum_{i=1}^{N} T(y_i)} \qquad (2.11)$$

Equation (2.11) is of course just another way of writing the aggregate revenue elasticity, but it can be useful in obtaining an analytical expression for the aggregate revenue elasticity.

Results corresponding to (2.2) and (2.4) for the individual case can also be obtained for $\eta_{T_Y,Y}$. Hence, denoting the aggregate effective average rate, $\sum_{i=1}^{N} T(y_i)/Y$, as ATR:

$$\eta_{T_Y,Y} = \frac{MTR}{ATR} = 1 + \eta_{ATR,Y} \qquad (2.12)$$

Furthermore:

$$\eta_{ATR,Y} = \sum_{i=1}^{N} \left\{ \frac{T(y_i)}{T_Y} \right\} \eta_{atr,y_i} \qquad (2.13)$$

Thus, a revenue–neutral increase in any η_{atr,y_i}, for which T_Y is constant, is necessarily associated with an increase in the aggregate revenue elasticity and hence in the aggregate effective marginal tax rate.

2.2.2 Non–equiproportional Income Changes

This subsection relaxes the assumption of equiproportionate income changes, used in the previous subsection and in the vast majority of studies. Lambert

(1993, pp. 209–212) provides a discussion of non–equiproportional growth. In line with the present approach of using parametric specifications at a fairly high level of aggregation, it is convenient to use a simple specification of the process of relative income change. As part of the process, it is also useful to impose random proportionate income changes, in addition to any systematic equalising or disequalising tendency. Without such changes, annual income inequality changes too rapidly. Consider the following dynamic process. Let y_{it} denote individual i's income in period t, and let μ_t denote the mean of logarithms in period t, with $g_t = \exp(\mu_t)$ as the geometric mean. The generating process can be written as:

$$y_{i2} = \left(\frac{y_{i1}}{g_1}\right)^{\beta} \exp(\mu_2 + u_i) \tag{2.14}$$

where u_i is $N(0, \sigma_u^2)$. The term β affects the degree of 'regression' away from or towards the (geometric) mean income. Where $\beta < 1$, those who are below the geometric mean experience, on average, proportionately larger income changes than those above the geometric mean. However, some people below the geometric mean may experience income reductions, depending on the size of the random component of income change. Equation (7.12) can be rewritten as:

$$(\log y_{i2} - \mu_2) = \beta (\log y_{i1} - \mu_1) + u_i \tag{2.15}$$

Hence the variance of logarithms of income in period 2, σ_2^2 , is given by:

$$\sigma_2^2 = \beta^2 \sigma_1^2 + \sigma_u^2 \tag{2.16}$$

If $\beta < 1$, the variance of logarithms is constant when $\sigma_u^2 = \sigma_1^2 (1 - \beta^2)$. In general, the variance of logarithms of income increases if the regression coefficient, β, exceeds the correlation between log–incomes in the two periods. If $\beta < 1$, the variance of logarithms of incomes eventually becomes stable at $\sigma_u^2/(1 - \beta^2)$. For further discussion of dynamic income specifications, see Creedy (1985).

2.3 The Multi–step Income Tax Function

The most common form of income tax function used in practice is the multi–step function. Not surprisingly, it has received most attention in the conceptual literature; see Hutton and Lambert (1980), Fries *et al.* (1982) and Caminada and Goudswaard (1996). Hence it is useful to examine this case closely. The multi–step tax function is described by a series of marginal tax rates and income thresholds over which the rates apply. Between two adjacent thresholds, the marginal tax rate is constant, giving the appearance of a step. Formally, the multi–step income tax function can be written as:

$$
\begin{aligned}
T\left(y_i\right) &= & 0 & & 0 < y_i \le a_1 \\
&= & t_1\left(y_i - a_1\right) & & a_1 < y_i \le a_2 \\
&= & t_1\left(a_2 - a_1\right) &+ t_2\left(y_i - a_2\right) & a_2 < y_i \le a_3
\end{aligned}
\tag{2.17}
$$

and so on.

If y_i falls into the kth tax bracket, so that $a_k < y_i \le a_{k+1}$, and $a_0 = t_0 = 0$, $T\left(y_i\right)$ can be written for $k \ge 1$ as:

$$
T\left(y_i\right) = t_k\left(y_i - a_k\right) + \sum_{j=0}^{k-1} t_j\left(a_{j+1} - a_j\right)
\tag{2.18}
$$

The expression for $T\left(y_i\right)$ in (2.18) can be rewritten as:

$$
T\left(y_i\right) = t_k y_i - \sum_{j=1}^{k} a_j\left(t_j - t_{j-1}\right)
\tag{2.19}
$$

Hence:

$$
T\left(y_i\right) = t_k\left(y_i - a_k'\right)
\tag{2.20}
$$

where:

$$
\begin{aligned}
a_k' &= a_k - \sum_{j=0}^{k-1}\left(\frac{t_j}{t_k}\right)\left(a_{j+1} - a_j\right) \\
&= \sum_{j=1}^{k} a_j\left(\frac{t_j - t_{j-1}}{t_k}\right)
\end{aligned}
\tag{2.21}
$$

The implication of (2.20) and (2.21) is that the tax function facing any individual taxpayer is equivalent to a tax function with a single marginal tax
rate, t_k, applied to income measured in excess of a single threshold, a'_k. The
term, a'_k, is the effective threshold for individuals in the kth class, and is
a weighted sum of the a_js, with weights, $(t_j - t_{j-1})/t_k$, determined by the
structure of marginal rate progression. Therefore, a'_k differs across individuals, unlike a_j, depending on the marginal income tax bracket, y_{ik}, into which
they fall. Strictly therefore $a'_k = a'_k(y_{ik})$ though to simplify presentation a'_k
is used here.

From (2.20), for $k \geq 1$, differentiation gives, for income changes which do
not involve a movement between tax brackets:

$$\eta_{T_y, y_i} = \frac{1 - da'_k/dy_i}{1 - a'_k/y_i} \qquad (2.22)$$

The term da'_k/dy_i allows for a change in the level of effective deductions
as y_i increases. Such a change is often thought of in the context of income
taxation though, as is shown in the next chapter, it is also relevant in the case
of consumption taxes where a change in income is associated with a change
in the proportion of total expenditure devoted to taxed goods. Writing $s_k =$
$a_{k+1} - a_k$ so that for $k \geq 1$, $a_k = \sum_{j=0}^{k-1} s_j$, and remembering that $a_0 = 0$, it
can be seen that $a'_k = \sum_{j=0}^{k-1} (1 - t_j/t_k) s_j$. In practice, as y_i increases the only
value of s that is likely to increase is $s_0 = a_1$, so that all other thresholds above
a_1 adjust accordingly. This arises where personal deductions are endogenous.
Hence $da'_k/dy_i = ds_0/dy_i = da_1/dy_i$.

Fries et al. (1982) show that changes in income-related deductions affect
estimates of US income tax revenue elasticities. For the simpler case where
$da'_k/dy_i = 0$, the elasticity becomes:

$$\eta_{T_y, y_i} = 1 + \frac{a'_k}{y_i - a'_k} \qquad (2.23)$$

The result in (2.23) can be compared with that in Hutton and Lambert (1983,
p. 224) who use a different terminology. They point out that the elasticity of

any tax, j, can be expressed as $\eta_j = 1 + K_j/T_j$, where T_j is the tax paid and K_j depends on the tax structure. The result in (2.23) can easily be rewritten in this general form, where K_j becomes $t_k a'_k$ and is an effective transfer payment, since net income is $t_k a'_k + y_i (1 - t_k)$. A corresponding result holds for all taxes combined such that $\eta = 1 + \sum_j K_j / \sum_j T_j$, where this aggregate elasticity is simply the tax–revenue–share weighted sum of the η_js. A change in the tax structure that is both revenue–neutral and elasticity–neutral must have $\triangle \sum_j T_j = \triangle \sum_j K_j = 0$.

Using the results in (2.4) and (2.23), it follows that $\eta_{atr,y_i} = -\eta_{T_y,a'_k} = a'_k / (y_i - a'_k)$. This shows that the elasticity of the average tax rate with respect to income is the negative of the elasticity of tax with respect to the effective threshold, which allows the tax elasticity for a multi–step function to be calculated solely from information on income levels and the effective allowance. This result does not appear to have been recognised in the existing conceptual literature or applied in practice.

Following Fries *et al.* (1982) the function, $T(y_i, a'_k)$ is homogeneous of degree 1, since $\theta T = T(\theta y_i, \theta a'_k)$. Hence from Euler's theorem:

$$T(y_i, a'_k) = y_i \frac{dT(y_i, a'_k)}{dy_i} + a'_k \frac{dT(y_i, a'_k)}{da'_k}$$

Dividing this throughout by T gives $\eta_{T_y,y_i} = 1 - \eta_{T_y,a'_k}$, where η_{T_y,a'_k} is the elasticity of income tax revenue with respect to a'_k. An increase in the effective threshold reduces taxable income, so that $\eta_{T_y,a'_k} < 0$. In the context of aggregate revenue, Fries *et al.* (1982) demonstrated a similar result for a multi–step function having a variety of allowances and income–related deductions; see also Lambert (1993, pp. 216–218).

To illustrate the properties of a multi–step function, suppose the rates and thresholds are as shown in the first two columns of Table 2.1, for a structure with $K = 4$. The associated values of a'_k are shown in the final column. For $y_i < a_1$ the elasticity is zero, since tax revenue remains constant at zero. As income crosses the a_1 threshold, the revenue elasticity becomes

Table 2.1: A Multi–step Tax Function

a_k	t_k	a'_k
5000	0.20	5000.00
15000	0.25	7000.00
25000	0.30	10000.00
40000	0.35	14285.71

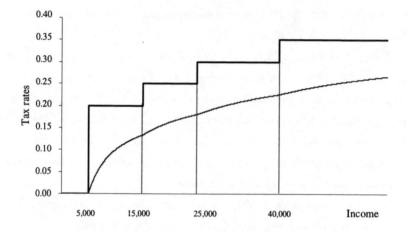

Figure 2.1: Marginal and Average Tax Rates

infinitely large, after which, for $a_1 < y_i < a_2$, it declines because, from (2.23),
$\eta_{T_y, y_i} = 1 + a_1 / (y_i - a_1)$. When $y_i = a_2$ the elasticity is:

$$\frac{t_2 a_2}{t_1 (a_2 - a_1)} \tag{2.24}$$

This is obtained by simplifying y_i multiplied by:

$$\frac{t_2 \left[1 + y_i - \left\{ a_2 - \frac{t_1}{t_2} (a_2 - a_1) \right\} \right]}{t_1 (y_i - a_1)} - 1 \tag{2.25}$$

where y_i is replaced by a_2. Appropriate expressions for higher thresholds can be obtained following the same procedure.

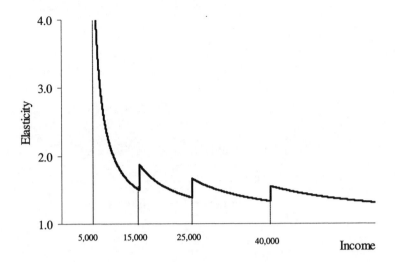

Figure 2.2: Tax Revenue Elasticity

The average and marginal rates for the tax structure in Table 2.1 are shown in Figure 2.1, and the variation in the revenue elasticity as y_i increases is illustrated in Figure 2.2.

Fries *et al.* (1982) and Hutton and Lambert (1983) note that it is possible to decompose the revenue elasticity, η_{T_y,y_i}, into components reflecting the effect on the tax base of a change in income, η_{B,y_i}, and the effect on tax payments of a change in the tax base, $\eta_{T_y,B}$, such that $\eta_{T_y,y_i} = \left(\eta_{T_y,B} \right) \left(\eta_{B,y_i} \right)$. In the multi–step income tax case, this translates to $B = y_i - a'_k$, $\eta_{T_y,B} = 1$, and:

$$\eta_{T_y,y_i} = \eta_{B,y_i} = 1 - \eta_{B,a'_k} = 1 - \eta_{T_y,a'_k} \qquad (2.26)$$

Finally, a summary of the results for individual revenue elasticities is given in Table 2.2.

Table 2.2: Individual Income Tax Elasticity

No.	Elasticity	Comments
	The general tax function	
1	$\frac{mtr_i}{atr_i}$	
2	$1 + \eta_{atr_i, y_i}$	
	The multi–step tax function	
3	$1 - \eta_{T_y, a'_k}$	a'_k = effective threshold
4	$1 - \eta_{B, a'_k}$	B = tax base: $(y - a'_k)$
5	$\frac{1 - \partial a'_k / \partial y_i}{1 - a'_k / y_i}$	No movements across tax brackets
6	$1 + \frac{a'_k}{y_i - a'_k}$	Assumes $\frac{\partial a'_k}{\partial y_i} = 0$
	The single–step tax function	
7	$1 + \frac{a}{y_i - a}$	a = tax-free threshold; $\frac{\partial a}{\partial y_i} = 0$

2.3.1   The Aggregate Elasticity

Section 2.2 showed, for the general case, how the aggregate revenue elasticity can be derived from the individual revenue elasticities. This demonstrated that the aggregate elasticity is a weighted average of the individual elasticities, with weights equal to the proportion of total revenue paid by each individual. Given that, in the case where the as are constant, the individual revenue elasticities exceed 1, the aggregate elasticity must also exceed 1.

This subsection examines the aggregate revenue elasticity for the multi–step income tax function introduced above. Suppose there are $K + 1$ tax brackets, such that $k = 0, 1, ..., K$, with $a_{K+1} = \infty$. For convenience, suppose there is a continuous income distribution function, $F(y)$, where $F(y)$ represents the proportion of people with income less than or equal to y, so that the summation over individuals in (2.11) is replaced by an integral and:

$$\eta_{T_Y,Y} = \frac{\int_0^\infty y T'(y)\, dF(y)}{\int_0^\infty T(y)\, dF(y)} \tag{2.27}$$

Using (2.20), aggregate tax revenue, T_Y, can be written as:

$$T_Y = N \sum_{k=1}^{K} \left[t_k \int_{a_k}^{a_{k+1}} (y - a_k')\, dF(y) \right] \tag{2.28}$$

This expression can be simplified further by noting that:

$$\int_{a_k}^{a_{k+1}} dF(y) = F(a_{k+1}) - F(a_k) \tag{2.29}$$

and:

$$\int_{a_k}^{a_{k+1}} y\, dF(y) = \bar{y}\{F_1(a_{k+1}) - F_1(a_k)\} \tag{2.30}$$

where $\bar{y}$ is arithmetic mean income and $F_1(.)$ denotes the first moment distribution function such that $F_1(y)$ is the proportion of total income obtained by those with income less than or equal to y; on the use of moment distributions in economics, see Hart (1975). Therefore $F_1(y) = \int_0^y u\, dF(u) / \int_0^\infty u\, dF(u)$

or $F_1(y) = \int_0^y u dF(u)/\bar{y}$. Thus:

$$T_Y = N\bar{y} \sum_{k=1}^{K} t_k \left[\{F_1(a_{k+1}) - F_1(a_k)\} - \frac{a'_k}{\bar{y}} \{F(a_{k+1}) - F(a_k)\} \right] \quad (2.31)$$

The first expression in curly brackets in equation (2.31) captures the proportion of total income between two adjacent thresholds, while the second expression in curly brackets is the proportion of people between the same thresholds. This may be written more succinctly by defining the function $G_k(a_k)$ as the term in square brackets in (2.31) so that:

$$T_Y = N\bar{y} \sum_{k=1}^{K} t_k G_k(a_k) \quad (2.32)$$

This gives the denominator of (2.11). The numerator is given by:

$$N \sum_{k=1}^{K} \left[t_k \int_{a_k}^{a_{k+1}} y dF(y) \right] \quad (2.33)$$

which, following the procedure used above, can be written as:

$$N\bar{y} \sum_{k=1}^{K} t_k \{F_1(a_{k+1}) - F_1(a_k)\} \quad (2.34)$$

which is the same as the first term in the denominator, in (2.31). The aggregate elasticity is then obtained simply by dividing (2.34) by (2.31). This can be arranged as the familiar form, for comparison with the individual revenue elasticities, of:

$$\eta_{T_Y,Y} = \frac{\bar{y}}{\bar{y} - a^*} = 1 + \frac{a^*}{\bar{y} - a^*} \quad (2.35)$$

where a^* is the effective aggregate allowance of:

$$a^* = \frac{\sum_{k=1}^{K} t_k a'_k \{F(a_{k+1}) - F(a_k)\}}{\sum_{k=1}^{K} t_k \{F_1(a_{k+1}) - F_1(a_k)\}} \quad (2.36)$$

Functions of the form $G(a)$ defined here play a prominent part in the analysis of tax and transfer systems; see Creedy (1996).

2.4   The Single–step Tax Function

A simplification of the result in (2.35) can be obtained for a single–step tax function, where there is a single marginal rate, $t = t_1$ above a tax–free threshold, $a = a_1$. Substitution in (2.32) gives the result that total revenue is:

$$T_Y = Nt\bar{y}G(a) \tag{2.37}$$

where:

$$G(a) = \{1 - F_1(a)\} - \left(\frac{a}{\bar{y}}\right)\{1 - F(a)\} \tag{2.38}$$

The term $G(a)$ may be compared with the corresponding term, $G_k(a_k)$, used in the multi–step function above. The result for the single–step function follows directly from that for the multi–step function by setting K equal to 1 in (2.31) and noting that $a_{K+1} = \infty$ and $F_1(\infty) = F(\infty) = 1$, while $a_1' = a$, so that in this case $G_1(a_1) = G(a)$.

The aggregate revenue elasticity, in (2.11), then requires the numerator, given by:

$$Nt \int_a^\infty y dF(y) = N\bar{y}t\{1 - F_1(a)\} \tag{2.39}$$

The aggregate elasticity takes precisely the same form as in equation (2.35), except that the effective threshold is given by $a^* = a\{1 - F(a)\}/\{1 - F_1(a)\}$.

In the special case where there is no one below a, $G(a) = 1 - a/\bar{y}$ and $a^* = a$, so that the elasticity becomes:

$$\eta_{T_Y,Y} = \frac{\bar{y}}{\bar{y} - a} = 1 + \frac{a}{\bar{y} - a} \tag{2.40}$$

This is independent of the marginal tax rate, t, and the form of the distribution of income. It is interesting to compare this result with that obtained by Hutton (1980), for the special case where incomes follow the Pareto distribution, whereby $f(y) = \alpha y_0^\alpha y^{-(1+\alpha)}$ for $y > y_0$, with $\alpha > 1$. Hutton showed that, irrespective of the form of the tax function, equiproportional income growth implies $\eta_{T_Y,Y} = \alpha$. At first sight this might seem to contradict (2.40),

Table 2.3: Aggregate Income Tax Elasticity

No.	Elasticity	Comments
	The general tax function	
1	$\dfrac{\sum_{i=1}^{N} y_i \eta_{y_i,Y} T'(y_i)}{\sum_{i=1}^{N} T(y_i)}$	$\eta_{y_i,Y}$ = elasticity of y_i w.r.t. Y
2	$\dfrac{\sum_{i=1}^{N} (y_i/Y) T'(y_i)}{\sum_{i=1}^{N} T(y_i)/Y}$	Cases 2–7: equiproportional income growth
3	$1 + \eta_{ATR,Y}$	
	The multi–step tax function	
4	$\sum_{i=1}^{N} \eta_{T_y,y_i} \dfrac{T\left(y_i, a'_k\right)}{T_Y}$	
5	$\dfrac{\sum_{i=1}^{N} y_i T'(y_i)}{\sum_{i=1}^{N} T(y_i)}$	
6	$1 + \dfrac{a^*}{\bar{y} - a^*}$	$\begin{cases} \bar{y} = \text{mean income} \\ a^* = \text{effective aggregate allowance} \end{cases}$
	The single–step tax function	
7	$1 + \dfrac{a}{\bar{y} - a}$	$y_i > a$ for all i

where the elasticity depends on the tax threshold (which is also the lowest income level) and $\bar{y}$, but otherwise does not depend on the form of the distribution. However, using the fact that $\bar{y} = \alpha y_0 / (\alpha - 1)$ for the Pareto distribution, and letting $a = y_0$, substitution into (2.40) confirms the Hutton result for the single–step case.

A summary of results for aggregate elasticities in the case of equiproportional income growth is given in Table 2.3.

2.5 Nonlinear Income Tax Functions

This section presents analytical results for two nonlinear income tax functions in the context of equi-proportional income changes.

2.5.1 A Five–parameter Function

It is sometimes useful to approximate a multi–step income tax function using the following nonlinear function involving five parameters:

$$
\begin{aligned}
T\left(y_i\right) &= 0 & y_i &\leq a_1 \\
&= t_1\left(y_i - a_1\right) & a_1 &< y_i \leq a_2 \\
&= t_1\left(a_2 - a_1\right) + \left(t_2 - hy_i^{-\beta}\right)\left(y_i - a_2\right) & y_i &> a_2
\end{aligned}
\tag{2.41}
$$

with $h = (t_2 - t_1)a_2^\beta$ and $\beta < 1$. Hence a standard rate of t_1 is applied to incomes between the thresholds a_1 and a_2, after which the marginal rate increases gradually up to a maximum of t_2. The condition $\beta < 1$ is required to ensure that the system is progressive and a higher value of β ensures that the marginal rates increase more rapidly. This nonlinear function was introduced by Creedy and Gemmell (1982), and used by Gemmell (1985). The aggregate revenue from this tax system is given by:

$$
T_Y = N\left[t_1\left\{G\left(1, a_1\right) - G\left(1, a_2\right)\right\} + t_2 G\left(1, a_2\right) - hG\left(1 - \beta, a_2\right)\right]
\tag{2.42}
$$

where the general function $G\left(r, a\right)$ is defined as:

$$
G\left(r, a\right) = \bar{y}_r\left[\left\{1 - F_r(a)\right\} - a\left(\frac{\bar{y}_{r-1}}{\bar{y}_r}\right)\left\{1 - F_{r-1}(a)\right\}\right]
\tag{2.43}
$$

and $\bar{y}_r$ denotes the rth moment about the origin so that, for example, $\bar{y}_1 = \bar{y}$. This expression therefore involves the concept of non-integer moment distribution functions. This function may be compared with the functions $G_k\left(a_k\right)$ and $G\left(a\right)$ introduced above. The numerator in the expression for the aggregate elasticity is then given by:

$$
Nt_1\int_{a_1}^{a_2} ydF\left(y\right) + N\int_{a_2}^{\infty} y\left\{t_2 - h\left(1 - k\right)y^{-k} - a_2khy^{-1-k}\right\}dF\left(y\right)
\tag{2.44}
$$

which can be simplified following the approach used above. Although the relevant expressions are slightly more awkward than in the case of the multi-step function, this nonlinear form is useful for examining wide variations in the form of the tax schedule using few parameters. It provides a good approximation to some schedules used in practice.

2.5.2 A Two–parameter Function

Suppose that the tax function takes the simple nonlinear form:

$$T\left(y_i\right) = y_i - \alpha y_i^\beta \tag{2.45}$$

where $\alpha, \beta > 0$ and $\beta < 2$ in order to ensure that the tax is progressive. This function is strictly limited to incomes above $\alpha^{a/(1-\beta)}$ in order to ensure that $T\left(y_i\right) > 0$, but this minimum is negligible. This function has been used in a number of contexts in which it is required to integrate income taxation into other economic models; for further references, see Creedy (1996, p. 50). Suppose also that incomes are lognormally distributed as $\Lambda\left(\mu, \sigma^2\right)$, where μ and σ^2 are respectively the mean and variance of logarithms of income. Hence:

$$\eta_{T_Y,Y} = \frac{\bar{y} - \alpha\beta \int y^\beta d\Lambda}{\bar{y} - \alpha \int y^\beta d\Lambda}. \tag{2.46}$$

Using the moment generating function of the normal distribution, $\int y^\beta d\Lambda = \exp\left(\beta\mu + \frac{1}{2}\beta^2\sigma^2\right)$, so that the aggregate revenue elasticity can be expressed as:

$$\eta_{T_Y,Y} = \frac{1 - \beta\Psi}{1 - \Psi} = 1 + \frac{\Psi\left(1 - \beta\right)}{1 - \Psi} \tag{2.47}$$

where:

$$\Psi = \alpha \exp\left\{\mu\left(\beta - 1\right) + \frac{1}{2}\left(\beta^2 - 1\right)\sigma^2\right\} \tag{2.48}$$

2.6 Calculation of Aggregate Elasticities

Previous sections have given a variety of expressions for aggregate income tax revenue elasticities. The question remains of how elasticities can be calculated in practice. In general the computation requires information about the distribution of income at any time, along with details of the dynamics of income change from one period to the next. The simplest case is of course where the income changes are assumed to be equi–proportional, that is where all values of $\eta_{y_i,Y}$ are unity. Here, the preferred approach depends on the available form of information about the income distribution.

First, suppose that a cross–sectional survey of a large number of individuals is available. In this case the individual values of η_{T_y,y_i} can be obtained from knowledge of the total tax paid (giving the average tax rate) and the marginal tax rate facing each person. The aggregate elasticity can be obtained as the tax–share weighted average of these individual elasticities. If it is required to project the aggregate elasticity, after a period of income growth, then for the equi–proportional case it is simply a matter of increasing each individual's income by the same amount and re–calculating the values of η_{T_y,y_i}, and so on.

Alternatively, data are often available only in the form of a grouped income distribution, or other summary information, such as several percentiles of the distribution. Such data may be used to estimate the parameters of a specified functional form to describe the distribution. Given the estimates, two approaches are available. First, a pseudo cross–sectional sample may be generated by taking a large number of random draws from the specified distribution, and then proceeding as described in the previous paragraph. This kind of simulation method has been used to investigate income tax revenue elasticities by, for example, Dorrington (1974), Spahn (1975) and Hutton and Lambert (1982b).

Second, knowledge of the form of the distribution can be used to obtain the required expressions given in subsection 2.3.1 and section 2.5. For example, suppose that incomes are lognormally distributed as $\Lambda\left(\mu, \sigma^2\right)$, where μ and σ^2 are respectively the mean and variance of logarithms of income. The parameters can be estimated using a variety of summary information; on the

Table 2.4: Calculating the Revenue Elasticity

a_k	t_k	a'_k	$F(a_k)$	$F_1(a_k)$	$G_k(a_k)$
5000	0.20	5000.00	0.0180	0.0025	0.0543
15000	0.25	7000.00	0.2935	0.1056	0.1245
25000	0.30	10000.00	0.5711	0.2987	0.1745
40000	0.35	14285.71	0.8006	0.5544	0.3449

lognormal distribution, see Aitchison and Brown (1957). The various terms required for the computation of the aggregate elasticity can be evaluated by making use of the convenient relationship between the moment distributions of the lognormal, whereby:

$$\Lambda_j \left(\mu, \sigma^2 \right) = \Lambda \left(\mu + j\sigma, \sigma^2 \right) \tag{2.49}$$

Suppose that μ and σ^2 are 10 and 0.5 respectively, producing an arithmetic mean income of $\bar{y} = \exp \left(\mu + \frac{1}{2}\sigma^2 \right) = 28,283$. Suppose also that $K = 4$, where the relevant thresholds and marginal rates are shown in the first two columns of Table 2.4. The remaining columns show the required information for calculating the aggregate elasticity. The effective marginal and average tax rates, and the revenue elasticity, are respectively 0.302, 0.215 and 1.402.

In the case of the multi–step tax function in Table 2.4, and the same lognormal distribution of income, a simulation of 5000 individuals from the distribution gives effective marginal and average rates of 0.302 and 0.215 respectively, along with an elasticity of 1.404; these values are very close to those obtained using the analytical expressions. The simulation method is necessary if it is required to examine the implications of non–equiproportional income growth, for which the analytic expressions become much more awkward to obtain.

2.7 Conclusions

This chapter has provided a unified framework in which to examine analytical expressions for the tax revenue elasticities of income taxes. The analytical results synthesised and extended here help to provide both an understanding of the determinants of the revenue responsiveness properties of different taxes and convenient expressions for the calculation of elasticities in practice. It can be seen that the magnitude of revenue elasticities can be expected to differ substantially for alternative forms of income tax, and for the same tax over time as, for example, incomes change relative to tax thresholds.

The various parameters in the tax elasticity expressions highlight a number of potential impacts of tax reform on revenue elasticities. For example, tax reforms are often undertaken to achieve particular revenue and/or redistributive objectives in the short–to–medium run, or to be revenue–neutral or distribution–neutral. However, it is less well appreciated that changes in tax progressivity often imply changes in elasticities, while (short–run) revenue–neutral changes are not necessarily elasticity–neutral. Many industrialised countries have undertaken significant tax reform in the last twenty years, often involving shifts towards less progressive income taxes and greater use of indirect taxes, as well as experiencing rising mean incomes relative to tax thresholds. Results here suggest that each of these changes can be expected to affect tax revenue elasticities, while commonly observed increases in the inequality of pre–tax incomes also affect these elasticities. Surprisingly, few attempts have been made to explore these issues empirically. The results presented here provide a foundation for such an analysis.

Chapter 3

Consumption Tax Revenue Elasticities

This chapter examines the built–in flexibility of consumptions taxes and combined income and consumption tax systems. It demonstrates that convenient analytical expressions can readily be obtained with the addition of relatively few parameters. The form of the expressions turn out to be similar to the more familiar formulae for income taxes, derived in the previous chapter. However, analytical results and numerical simulations suggest that, unlike income taxes, consumption tax revenues are likely to be income–inelastic in practice, and the built–in flexibility of a combined income–consumption tax system, though typically elastic, can be expected to decline over time in the absence of countervailing fiscal reforms. These results also provide some insight into the longer term effects on tax revenues, often unintended or unknown, of fiscal reforms, such as changes to income tax progressivity or increased use of indirect taxes, which are often made with other policy objectives in mind.

The chapter is organised as follows. Since consumption tax revenues derive from expenditures out of disposable income, it is necessary to begin by specifying the income tax system in Section 3.1. Section 3.2 then extends the analysis to include *ad valorem* and unit consumption taxes. In section 3.3 the implications for the revenue elasticity of changes in indirect tax rates

41

are examined, and section 3.4 extends the analysis of revenue elasticities for an individual to the aggregate revenue elasticity across all individuals. Some illustrative calculations based on the Australian income and consumption tax system are reported in section 3.5. Section 3.6 briefly concludes.

3.1   Allowing for Income Taxation

To derive expressions for the consumption tax revenue elasticity this chapter adopts the multi–step income tax function defined in chapter 2 by:

$$
\begin{aligned}
T_y(y_i) &= 0 & 0 < y_i \le a_1 \\
&= t_1\,(y_i - a_1) & a_1 < y_i \le a_2 \\
&= t_1\,(a_2 - a_1) \;+\; t_2\,(y_i - a_2) & a_2 < y_i \le a_3
\end{aligned}
\tag{3.1}
$$

and so on. As chapter 2 demonstrated, this is equivalent to a single–step income tax given by:

$$
T_y(y_i) = t_k\,(y_i - a'_k)
\tag{3.2}
$$

where:

$$
a'_k = \sum_{j=1}^{k} a_j \left(\frac{t_j - t_{j-1}}{t_k} \right)
\tag{3.3}
$$

Equation (3.2) specifies a single marginal tax rate, t_k, applied to income measured in excess of a single effective threshold, a'_k. The individual revenue elasticity of income taxes associated with this tax function was shown in chapter 2 to be:

$$
\eta_{T_y, y_i} = \frac{1 - da'_k/dy_i}{1 - a'_k/y_i} = \frac{y_i - a'_k \eta_{a'_k, y_i}}{y_i - a'_k} = 1 + \left(\frac{a'_k}{y_i - a'_k} \right)(1 + \eta_{a'_k, y_i})
\tag{3.4}
$$

The term $\eta_{a'_k, y_i}$ captures the impact on the revenue elasticity, in unit–free terms, of changes in effective deductions as y_i increases. In many income tax systems, tax thresholds are fixed (though they may be determined by personal characteristics such as age or marital status), such that $\eta_{a'_k, y_i} = 0$. In other cases, for example the UK, this term plays an important role. However, in the case of consumption taxes, there is generally an equivalent non–zero elasticity because, as shown below, a change in income is typically associated with a change in the proportion of total expenditure devoted to taxed goods. Thus the amount of spending that is free from expenditure tax varies with the individual's income or total expenditure.

3.2 Consumption Taxes

Having specified the income tax system, this section extends the analysis to include consumption tax revenue. This is complicated by the need to allow for consumers' responses to changes in disposable income. Analytical expressions are obtained for the tax revenue elasticities of both *ad valorem* and unit consumption taxes. Elasticity expressions for combined income and consumption tax revenues are also obtained. As later chapters demonstrate, in many cases these revenue elasticities can be calculated using limited information on expenditure patterns in addition to data on the tax parameters.

Consider an individual with income of y_i and facing the multi–step income tax function in equation (3.2). This determines the individual's disposable income $z_i = y_i - T(y_i)$. For many individuals, savings represent a non–negligible fraction of their disposable income. Let γ_i be the fraction of disposable income devoted to expenditure by individual i, with $(1 - \gamma_i)$ the fraction of disposable income saved. In general, γ_i can be expected to vary with z_i, reflecting different individuals' propensities to save. In addition, some individuals, such as those on low incomes, may be in receipt of transfer payments which typically serve to raise expenditure relative to post–income–tax income.

Define consumption expenditure by individual i, m_i, as:

$$m_i = \gamma_i z_i \qquad (3.5)$$

Thus, from (3.5), consumption expenditure is given by:

$$m_i = \gamma_i \left\{ a'_k t_k + y_i \left(1 - t_k \right) \right\} \tag{3.6}$$

To simplify the exposition initally savings are ignored, such that $\gamma_i = 1$, and $m_i = z_i = a'_k t_k + y_i \left(1 - t_k \right)$. The next three subsections consider the cases of multiple *ad valorum* rates, a uniform tax rate, and a two–rate structure, when there are no savings. The effects of including savings are then examined in subsection 3.2.4.

3.2.1   Multiple Indirect Tax Rates

Suppose that the tax–exclusive *ad valorem* indirect tax rate imposed on the ℓth good (for $\ell = 1, ..., n$) is v_ℓ, giving rise to the equivalent tax–inclusive rate of $v'_\ell = v_\ell / \left(1 + v_\ell \right)$. Any indirect taxes that are not imposed as *ad valorem* rates can be expressed as equivalent to *ad valorem* rates. For example, a unit tax of $t_{u\ell}$ imposed on the tax–exclusive price, $p_{E\ell}$, of the ℓth good, yields the tax–inclusive price of $p_\ell = p_{E\ell} + t_{u\ell}$, which is equivalent to an *ad valorem* rate of $\left(t_{u\ell}/p_\ell \right) / \left(1 - t_{u\ell}/p_\ell \right)$.

Defining w_ℓ as the budget share of the ℓth good, $m_{i\ell}/m_i$, the consumption tax paid by i on all $\ell = 1, ..., n$ goods, $T_v(y_i)$, is given by:

$$T_v(y_i) = m_i \sum_{\ell=1}^{n} v'_\ell w_{i\ell} \tag{3.7}$$

The total consumption and income tax paid by the individual, $R\left(y_i \right)$, is therefore given by:

$$
\begin{aligned}
R\left(y_i \right) &= T_y(y_i) + T_v(y_i) \tag{3.8} \\
&= t_k \left(y_i - a'_k \right) + \left\{ a'_k t_k + y_i \left(1 - t_k \right) \right\} \sum_{\ell=1}^{n} v'_\ell w_{i\ell} \tag{3.9}
\end{aligned}
$$

For simplicity, consider the case where the income tax thresholds are fixed, so that $\eta_{a'_k, y_i} = 0$ in equation (3.4). This assumption is readily relaxed, as shown below. Then the change in total revenue resulting from an increase in the individual's income, assuming that the individual does not move into a higher tax bracket, is given by:

$$\frac{dR\left(y_i\right)}{dy_i} = t_k + \left(1 - t_k\right) \sum_{\ell=1}^{n} v_\ell' w_{i\ell} + m_i \sum_{\ell=1}^{n} v_\ell' \frac{dw_{i\ell}}{dy_i} \qquad (3.10)$$

The last term in (3.10) involves changes in budget shares as income increases. In order to obtain a convenient expression for $dw_{i\ell}/dy_i$, first use the fact that, if e_ℓ is the total expenditure elasticity of demand for the ℓth good:

$$e_\ell = \frac{dm_{i\ell}/m_{i\ell}}{dm_i/m_i} = 1 + \frac{dw_{i\ell}/w_{i\ell}}{dm_i/m_i} \qquad (3.11)$$

so that:

$$\frac{dw_{i\ell}}{dm_i} = \frac{w_\ell\left(e_{i\ell} - 1\right)}{m_i} \qquad (3.12)$$

Then write:

$$\frac{dw_{i\ell}}{dy_i} = \frac{dw_{i\ell}}{dm_i}\frac{dm_i}{dy_i} \qquad (3.13)$$

so that by using $dm_i/dy_i = 1 - t_k$ from (3.6), it can be seen that:

$$\frac{dw_{i\ell}}{dy_i} = \frac{w_{i\ell}\left(e_{i\ell} - 1\right)\left(1 - t_k\right)}{m_i} \qquad (3.14)$$

Substituting the right–hand side of (3.14) into (3.10) and rearranging gives:

$$\frac{dR\left(y_i\right)}{dy_i} = t_k + \left(1 - t_k\right) \sum_{\ell=1}^{n} v_\ell' w_{i\ell} e_{i\ell} \qquad (3.15)$$

Finally, multiply (3.15) by $y_i/R(y_i)$, where $R(y_i)$ is given by (3.9), and the total income plus consumption tax revenue elasticity, η_{R,y_i}, is found to be:

$$\eta_{R,y_i} = \frac{1 + \frac{1-t_k}{t_k} \sum_{\ell=1}^{n} v_\ell' w_{i\ell} e_{i\ell}}{1 - \frac{a_k'}{y_i}\left(1 - \sum_{\ell=1}^{n} v_\ell' w_{i\ell}\right) + \frac{1-t_k}{t_k} \sum_{\ell=1}^{n} v_\ell' w_{i\ell}} \qquad (3.16)$$

The expression for η_{R,y_i} in (3.16) looks rather cumbersome but can be simplified by noting from (3.2) that the marginal rate of income tax, $mtr_y =$

$dT_y(y_i)/dy_i$, is equal to t_k, and the average rate of income tax, atr_y, is given by:

$$atr_y = \frac{T_y(y_i)}{y_i} = t_k \left(1 - \frac{a'_k}{y_i}\right) \tag{3.17}$$

After some re–arranging, this allows (3.16) to be expressed as:

$$\eta_{R,y_i} = \frac{mtr_y + (1 - mtr_y) \sum_{\ell=1}^{n} v'_\ell w_{i\ell} e_{i\ell}}{atr_y + (1 - atr_y) \sum_{\ell=1}^{n} v'_\ell w_{i\ell}} \tag{3.18}$$

In (3.18) the marginal and average rates of income tax have three effects. Firstly, higher rates affect the total revenue elasticity directly since the income tax revenue elasticity is simply mtr_y/atr_y. An increase in mtr_y, for example, raises atr_y via changes in a'_k. However, the effect on atr_y is less than proportional so that the overall effect is to increase the income tax elasticity.

Secondly higher income tax rates simultaneously reduce the total revenue elasticity by reducing expenditure available to be taxed via indirect taxes, as captured by the terms in $(1 - mtr_y)$ and $(1 - atr_y)$. Thirdly, there is a compositional effect via changes in the share of income tax in total tax revenue. Expressing the combined tax revenue elasticity in terms of mtr_y and atr_y also allows (3.18) to be used for the case where $\eta_{a'_k,y_i} \neq 0$. In this case mtr_y becomes, from (3.2), $mtr_y = t_k(1 - da'_k/dy_i)$ and atr_y is unchanged as in (3.17).

Further insight into the roles played by the various components in the η_{R,y_i} expressions in (3.16) and (3.18) can be gained by decomposing η_{R,y_i} into its income and consumption tax components. Thus, η_{R,y_i} is the weighted average of the elasticities for income and consumption taxes, η_{T_y,y_i} and η_{T_v,y_i} respectively; that is

$$\eta_{R,y_i} = \left(\frac{T_v}{R}\right) \eta_{T_v,y_i} + \left(\frac{T_y}{R}\right) \eta_{T_y,y_i} \tag{3.19}$$

where the weights are the shares of each tax in total tax revenue. The income tax elasticity, η_{T_y,y_i}, was given in equation (3.4) and shown in chapter 2 to be equal to mtr_y/atr_y. It can be shown that the contribution of the consumption tax elasticity to (3.16) is given by:

$$\eta_{T_v,y_i} = \frac{\left(\frac{1-t_k}{t_k}\right) \sum_{\ell=1}^{n} v'_\ell w_{i\ell} e_{i\ell}}{\left(\frac{a'_k}{y_i} + \frac{1-t_k}{t_k}\right) \sum_{\ell=1}^{n} v'_\ell w_{i\ell}} \tag{3.20}$$

Alternatively, in terms of marginal and average income tax rates, (3.20) can be expressed as:

$$\eta_{T_v,y_i} = \frac{(1 - mtr_y) \sum_{\ell=1}^{n} v'_\ell w_{i\ell} e_{i\ell}}{(1 - atr_y) \sum_{\ell=1}^{n} v'_\ell w_{i\ell}} \tag{3.21}$$

In fact, the elasticity in (3.21) can be further simplified by noting that the term:

$$\frac{\sum_{\ell=1}^{n} v'_\ell w_{i\ell} e_{i\ell}}{\sum_{\ell=1}^{n} v'_\ell w_{i\ell}} = \sum_{\ell=1}^{n} \left(\frac{v'_\ell w_{i\ell}}{\sum_{\ell=1}^{n} v'_\ell w_{i\ell}}\right) e_{i\ell}$$

$$= \sum_{\ell=1}^{n} \left(\frac{v'_\ell w_{i\ell} m_i}{\sum_{\ell=1}^{n} v'_\ell w_{i\ell} m_i}\right) e_{i\ell}$$

$$= \sum_{\ell=1}^{n} \left(\frac{T_{i\ell}}{T_{v_i}}\right) e_{i\ell} \tag{3.22}$$

so that, substitution into (3.21) gives:

$$\eta_{T_v,y_i} = \left(\frac{1 - mtr_y}{1 - atr_y}\right) \sum_{\ell=1}^{n} \left(\frac{T_{i\ell}}{T_{v_i}}\right) e_{i\ell} \tag{3.23}$$

where $\sum_{\ell=1}^{n} (T_{i\ell}/T_{v_i}) e_{i\ell}$ in (3.23) is simply the tax–share weighted sum of the expenditure elasticities for taxed goods

These results show that the evaluation of η_{R,y_i} requires, in addition to the tax parameters, information about individuals' budget shares (or indirect tax shares) and the total expenditure elasticity of demand for each good. This information can generally be obtained from cross–sectional household budget surveys. As the next two subsections show, in the case of indirect tax systems which adopt greater uniformity of tax rates across goods, elasticity expressions become simpler and easier to estimate in practice.

3.2.2   Uniform Tax Rates

The results in (3.18) and (3.23) can be applied to any structure of indirect tax rates, but consider the special case where $v'_\ell = v'$ for all ℓ. Using the additivity properties that $\sum_{\ell=1}^n w_{i\ell} e_{i\ell} = \sum_{\ell=1}^n w_{i\ell} = 1$, the combined revenue elasticity becomes:

$$\eta_{R,y_i} = 1 + \frac{a'_k}{\Omega y_i - a'_k} \tag{3.24}$$

where:

$$\Omega = \frac{1}{1 - v'} + \left(\frac{v'}{1 - v'}\right)\left(\frac{1 - t_k}{t_k}\right) \tag{3.25}$$

or, using (3.18):

$$\eta_{R,y_i} = \frac{mtr_y + (1 - mtr_y)\, v'}{atr_y + (1 - atr_y)\, v'} \tag{3.26}$$

It can be seen that $\Omega > 1$, so that comparison of η_{R,y_i} in (3.24) with η_{T_y,y_i} in (3.4) reveals that the latter must exceed the former. Hence, overall tax revenue is less elastic than income tax revenue, remembering that (3.24) is derived using the assumption that $\eta_{a'_k,y_i} = 0$.

For the consumption tax revenue elasticity in this special case, substitution of $v'_\ell = v'$ into (3.21) gives:

$$\eta_{T_v,y_i} = 1 - \frac{a'_k}{\left(\frac{1 - t_k}{t_k}\right) y_i + a'_k} = 1 - \frac{t_k a'_k}{m_i} \tag{3.27}$$

where $t_k a'_k$ is the effective allowance. Substituting the expressions for mtr_y and atr_y obtained in the previous subsection into (3.27) gives, after some re-arranging:

$$\eta_{T_v,y_i} = \left(\frac{1 - mtr_y}{1 - atr_y}\right) \tag{3.28}$$

It can be seen that, with uniform indirect tax rates, only the *income tax* parameters are relevant for the consumption tax revenue elasticity, and $0 < \eta_{T_v,y_i} < 1$ in the presence of a progressive income tax, for which $mtr_y > atr_y$. However, as (3.24) shows, inelastic consumption tax revenue cannot outweigh the elastic responsiveness of income taxes, given in (3.4), such that total revenue remains income elastic: hence $\eta_{R,y_i} > 1$.

While the uniform rate case produces particularly simple elasticity expressions, the special case of a two–rate structure is of more policy relevance, and is examined in the following subsection.

3.2.3 The Two–rate Case

Consider the common situation where a subset of goods is untaxed, or taxed at a zero rate, while others are taxed at a common rate, v'. In a value–added type of tax system, a distinction must of course be made between tax exempt and zero–rated goods, but this can be ignored here. If goods are ordered such that the first s goods have a zero rate, the consumption tax revenue, $T_v(y_i)$, is:

$$T_v(y_i) = v'm_i \left(1 - \sum_{\ell=1}^{s} w_{i\ell} \right) \tag{3.29}$$

The term in brackets in (3.29) is the proportion of expenditure on taxed goods. This kind of zero–rating is usually imposed in order to introduce some progressivity into the indirect tax structure, by selecting the first s goods to be those where budget shares decline as total expenditure increases.

Letting $w^* = \sum_{\ell=1}^{s} w_{i\ell}$ denote the proportion of total expenditure devoted to untaxed goods, differentiation of (3.29) gives:

$$\frac{dT_v(y_i)}{dm_i} = v'(1 - w^*) - v'm_i \frac{\partial w^*}{\partial m_i} \tag{3.30}$$

From (3.12), $\partial w^*/\partial m_i$ can be written as:

$$\frac{\partial w^*}{\partial m_i} = \frac{\sum_{\ell=1}^{s} (e_{i\ell} w_{i\ell} - w_{i\ell})}{m_i} = \frac{(e^* - w^*)}{m_i} \tag{3.31}$$

where $e^* = \sum_{\ell=1}^{s} e_{i\ell} w_{i\ell}$. Hence, e^* is a budget–share weighted sum of the total expenditure (income) elasticities of those goods for which the tax rate is zero. Using (3.31) to substitute for $\partial w^*/\partial m_i$ in (3.30) gives:

$$\frac{dT_v(y_i)}{dm_i} = v'(1 - e^*) \tag{3.32}$$

and the consumption tax revenue elasticity at the individual level with respect to total expenditure, η_{T_v,m_i}, is:

$$\eta_{T_v,m_i} = \frac{1 - e^*}{1 - w^*} \tag{3.33}$$

This elasticity takes the familiar form that might be expected from (3.4). In (3.33) e^* captures the effect of endogenous changes in zero–rated expenditures (analogous to da'_k/dy_i in (3.4)) and w^* is the proportion of untaxed expenditure (analogous to a'_k/y_i in (3.4)). In the trivial case where all goods are zero–rated, then $n = s$ and $e^* = 1$, so that, as expected, the elasticity is zero. The denominator is simply the proportion of total expenditure that is subject to taxation, while the numerator is the (budget–share weighted) sum of the total expenditure elasticities of the taxed goods. Since the budget–share weighted sum of the elasticities of *all* goods must equal unity, that is $\sum_{\ell=1}^{n} e_{i\ell}w_{i\ell} = 1$, it follows that $1 - e^* = \sum_{\ell=1}^{n} e_{i\ell}w_{i\ell} - \sum_{\ell=1}^{s} e_{i\ell}w_{i\ell} = \sum_{\ell=s+1}^{n} e_{i\ell}w_{i\ell}$ and $1 - w^* = \sum_{\ell=s+1}^{n} w_{i\ell}$.

The numerator of (3.33) can also be expressed as $(1 - w^*) - m_i (\partial w^*/\partial m_i)$, such that it becomes:

$$\eta_{T_v,m_i} = 1 - \frac{m_i (\partial w^*/\partial m_i)}{1 - w^*} \tag{3.34}$$

where $m_i (\partial w^*/\partial m_i)$ reflects the endogenous change in zero–rated expenditure (equivalent to an effective allowance) as total expenditure rises.

In order to obtain the income elasticity of indirect tax, it is necessary to use the multiplicative property of elasticities. Any elasticity can be written as the product of the effect on tax payments of a change in the tax base and the effect on the tax base of a change in income. The consumption tax revenue elasticity can thus be written as $\eta_{T_v,y_i} = \eta_{T_v,m_i}\eta_{m_i,y_i}$, and using the result that $\eta_{m_i,y_i} = (1 - t_k) y_i/m_i$, it can be found that:

$$\eta_{T_v,y_i} = \frac{y_i (1 - t_k) (1 - e^*)}{m_i (1 - w^*)} \tag{3.35}$$

where the denominator is taxed expenditure. Further insight can be gained by making use of the fact that $m_i = a'_k t_k + y_i (1 - t_k)$, to rewrite (3.35) as:

$$
\begin{aligned}
\eta_{T_v, y_i} &= \left(1 - \frac{a'_k t_k}{m_i}\right) \left(\frac{1 - e^*}{1 - w^*}\right) \\
&= \left(\frac{1 - mtr_y}{1 - atr_y}\right) \left(\frac{1 - e^*}{1 - w^*}\right) \quad (3.36)
\end{aligned}
$$

From (3.36) it can be seen that a higher total expenditure elasticity of demand for zero–rated goods, e^*, implies a lower revenue elasticity, while a higher proportion of total expenditure devoted to zero–rated goods, w^*, is associated with a higher revenue elasticity. The first property is intuitively clear, since a higher elasticity implies that consumption moves more rapidly away from untaxed goods as disposable income rises; in practice, zero–rated goods are likely to have relatively low elasticities. The second property suggests that a policy change which reduces the number of zero–rated goods, in order to increase tax revenue initially, has the effect of reducing the revenue elasticity, thereby reducing revenue growth.

Equation (3.36) also indicates the conditions under which the consumption tax revenue is elastic or inelastic. Consider the two multiplicative terms in brackets in (3.36). The former, $(1 - mtr_y) / (1 - atr_y)$, is determined by the progressivity of the income tax and must be less than unity for a progressive tax: $mtr_y > atr_y$. The second term, $(1 - e^*) / (1 - w^*)$, reflects the progressivity of the consumption tax, as captured by the expenditure elasticities of the zero–rated goods, e_ℓ. Where only necessities are zero–rated ($e_\ell < 1$ for all $\ell = 1, ..., s$) it can be shown that $(1 - e^*) > (1 - w^*)$. From the definitions of e^* and w^*, it can be found that:

$$
\frac{1 - e^*}{1 - w^*} = \frac{1 - \sum_{\ell=1}^{s} e_\ell w_\ell}{1 - \sum_{\ell=1}^{s} w_\ell} \quad (3.37)
$$

A sufficient condition for this to exceed unity is therefore that all $e_\ell < 1$ ($\ell = 1, ..., s$). The necessary condition is that the budget–share weighted elasticity of taxed goods, $1 - e^*$, exceeds the sum of their budget shares.

Thus, within the subset of zero–rated goods, provided those with inelastic demands dominate (in terms of budget shares) those with elastic demands, $(1 - e^*) / (1 - w^*)$ exceeds unity. Thus in (3.36) greater progressivity of the income tax exerts an inelastic influence on the consumption tax revenue elasticity while greater progressivity of the consumption tax exerts an elastic influence. The overall outcome is ambiguous.

In some cases it may be possible to specify $w^* = \sum_{\ell=1}^{s} w_\ell$ directly as a function, say $r\left(m_i\right)$, of total expenditure. In the simple, though not realistic, case where the proportion of zero-rated expenditure is inversely proportional to total expenditure, so that $r\left(m_i\right) = \alpha/m_i$, then $T_v\left(y_i\right) = v'\left(m_i - \alpha\right)$. Here the use of zero–rated goods acts as a fixed allowance against total expenditure. The reciprocal case was implicit in Kay and Morris (1979) while a double–log specification was used by Creedy and Gemmell (1984, 1985) and Gemmell (1985), and this was extended so that $r\left(m\right)$ takes a finite value when $m = 0$, in Creedy (1992).

Finally, the total income–plus–consumption tax revenue elasticity can be obtained for this two–rate case by using:

$$R(y_i) = t_k \left(y_i - a'_k\right) + m_i v'(1 - w^*) \tag{3.38}$$

hence:

$$\frac{dR\left(y_i\right)}{dy_i} = t_k + (1 - t_k)\, v'(1 - w^*) - m_i v' \left(\frac{dw^*}{dm_i}\frac{dm_i}{dy_i}\right) \tag{3.39}$$

After some manipulation, it can be shown that the total tax revenue elasticity is given by:

$$\eta_{R,y_i} = \frac{mtr_y + (1 - mtr_y)\, v'(1 - e^*)}{atr_y + (1 - atr_y)\, v'(1 - w^*)} \tag{3.40}$$

This may be compared with the more general case of equation (3.18).

3.2.4   Allowing for Savings

Allowing for the possibility that not all disposable income is consumed is readily incorporated into the analysis of previous subsections to show how elasticity expressions differ when some disposable income is saved.

Using the definition of expenditure by individual i, in (3.5), this section relaxes the assumption that $\gamma_i = 1$, so that

$$m_i = \gamma_i z_i = \gamma_i \{y_i - T(y_i, a'_k)\} \tag{3.41}$$

It was shown in subsection 3.2.1 that an important component of the consumption tax and combined income–plus–consumption tax elasticities is the budget share–income differential, given by:

$$\frac{dw_{i\ell}}{dy_i} = \frac{dw_{i\ell}}{dm_i} \frac{dm_i}{dy_i} \tag{3.42}$$

Using (3.12) and (3.41) $\frac{dw_{i\ell}}{dy_i}$ can be redefined as:

$$
\begin{aligned}
\frac{dw_{i\ell}}{dy_i} &= \frac{dw_{i\ell}}{dm_i} \left\{ \frac{\partial m_i}{\partial y_i} + \frac{\partial m_i}{\partial \gamma_i} \frac{\partial \gamma_i}{\partial y_i} \right\} \\
&= \frac{w_{i\ell}(e_{i\ell}-1)}{m_i} \left\{ \gamma_i(1-t_k) + (a'_k t_k + y_i(1-t_k)) \frac{\partial \gamma_i}{\partial y_i} \right\}
\end{aligned} \tag{3.43}
$$

This reduces to equation (3.14) for a constant $\gamma_i = 1$. The effect of savings on the revenue elasticities therefore depends on the size of γ_i and the size and sign of $\partial \gamma_i / \partial y_i$. For an individual whose income rises within the income distribution, $\partial \gamma_i / \partial y_i < 0$ might be expected if savings rates increase with incomes. However, for incomes in aggregate, evidence suggests that for a proportionate increase in all incomes, $\partial \gamma / \partial Y = 0$ is appropriate. It is the latter which is typically the more relevant for empirical estimates of revenue elasticities.

For the case where $\gamma_i < 1$ but $\partial \gamma_i / \partial y_i = 0$, it is readily shown that the consumption tax revenue elasticity in equation (3.21) becomes:

$$
\begin{aligned}
\eta_{T_v, y_i} &= \frac{\gamma_i(1-t_k) y_i \sum_{\ell=1}^n v'_\ell w_{i\ell} e_{i\ell}}{m_i \sum_{\ell=1}^n v'_\ell w_{i\ell}} \\
&= \frac{(1-t_k) y_i \sum_{\ell=1}^n v'_\ell w_{i\ell} e_{i\ell}}{z_i \sum_{\ell=1}^n v'_\ell w_{i\ell}}
\end{aligned} \tag{3.44}
$$

or alternatively:

$$\eta_{T_v, y_i} = \frac{(1 - mtr_y) \sum_{\ell=1}^{n} v'_\ell w_{i\ell} e_{i\ell}}{(1 - atr_y) \sum_{\ell=1}^{n} v'_\ell w_{i\ell}} \tag{3.45}$$

so that, as a comparison of (3.44) with (3.20) shows, the elasticity is unaffected by the existance of savings provided disposable income, z_i, rather than consumption, m_i, appears in the denominator. Where $\partial \gamma_i / \partial y_i < 0$ then it can be shown that (3.21) generalises to:

$$\eta_{T_v, y_i} = \frac{\left\{ (1 - t_k)(y_i/z_i) + \eta_{\gamma_i, y_i} \right\} \sum_{\ell=1}^{n} v'_\ell w_{i\ell} e_{i\ell}}{\sum_{\ell=1}^{n} v'_\ell w_{i\ell}} \tag{3.46}$$

Substituting in (3.46) again using the definitions for mtr_y and atr_y derived in subsection 3.2.1, it can be shown that (3.46) becomes:

$$
\begin{aligned}
\eta_{T_v, y_i} &= \left(\eta_{\gamma_i, y_i} + \frac{1 - mtr_{y_i}}{1 - atr_{y_i}} \right) \left\{ \sum_{\ell=1}^{n} \left(\frac{T_{i\ell}}{T_{v_i}} \right) e_{i\ell} \right\} \\
&= (1 + \eta_{\gamma_i, z_i}) \left(\frac{1 - mtr_{y_i}}{1 - atr_{y_i}} \right) \left\{ \sum_{\ell=1}^{n} \left(\frac{T_{i\ell}}{T_{v_i}} \right) e_{i\ell} \right\}
\end{aligned}
\tag{3.47}
$$

Thus, if $\eta_{\gamma_i, z_i} < 0$, that is the savings proportion increases with disposable income, it can be seen from (3.46) that the consumption tax revenue elasticity is lower than the comparable case in (3.23). In this case savings act in a similar manner to the progressive income tax, lowering the consumption tax revenue elasticity. A converse result applies if higher savings rates are associated with lower income levels: $\eta_{\gamma_i, z_i} > 0$. The first two bracketed terms of equation (3.47) are less than or equal to unity, provided $\eta_{\gamma_i, z_i} < 0$, and the income tax is progressive. The third component, shown in curly brackets, may exceed unity for some income levels and tax structures. However, η_{T_v, y_i} tends towards unity as income increases. This is because all expenditure elasticities converge towards unity, along with the first two terms in (3.47), although the convergence may not be monotonic.

The elasticity of total income plus consumption tax revenue is affected by the inclusion of savings, even in the case where $\partial \gamma_i / \partial y_i = 0$. This occurs via compositional effects since, *ceteris paribus*, the share of consumption tax revenue in total tax revenue will be lower for $\gamma_i < 1$ than when $\gamma_i = 1$; see (3.19). Thus it is readily shown that, where $\gamma_i < 1$, equation (3.18) becomes:

$$\eta_{R,y_i} = \frac{mtr_y + (1 - mtr_y)\,\gamma_i \sum_{\ell=1}^{n} v'_\ell w_{i\ell} e_{i\ell}}{atr_y + (1 - atr_y)\,\gamma_i \sum_{\ell=1}^{n} v'_\ell w_{i\ell}}. \tag{3.48}$$

It is not immediately obvious from (3.48) whether $\gamma_i < 1$ serves to raise or lower the revenue elasticity compared to the case of no savings where $\gamma_i = 1$; this depends on whether the proportionate reduction in the numerator or denominator of (3.48) is greater. However, with the share of consumption tax revenue lower in this case (in comparison with $\gamma_i = 1$) and an income tax revenue elasticity which typically exceeds that for consumption taxes, it can be expected that the overall revenue elasticity in (3.48) typically exceeds that in the 'no savings' case in (3.18).

This section therefore demonstrates that where savings are proportional to income, such that $\eta_{\gamma_i,y_i} = 0$, the revenue elasticity of consumption taxes is unaffected but the combined income–plus–consumption tax revenue elasticity is affected via compositional effects from the two taxes. When savings are non–proportionally related to income, in particular where saving rates rise with income levels, this generates effects on expenditure similar to those from a progressive income tax, thus tending to reduce consumption tax revenue elasticities. However, though the cross–sectional consumption function may be non–proportional, what matters here when incomes are growing over time is whether saving rates tend to rise over time with incomes or remain constant. If the latter holds, then $\gamma_i < 1$ combined with $\eta_{\gamma_i,y_i} = 0$ is the relevant case for estimates of revenue elasticities.

The various results derived in this, and previous, subsections are summarised in Table 3.1. This reveals both the apparent complexity of the revenue elasticity when consumption tax rates vary across goods and the simplifications made possible when uniform or two–rate cases are appropriate and when savings rates are proportional to income. However, even in the more complex cases, the information requirements to enable elasticities to be

Table 3.1: Elasticity Expressions for Consumption Taxes

No.	Tax Function	Elasticity	Comments
	Consumption Tax: η_{T_v, y_i}		m_i = expenditure
1	M–step: ad val. rates v_ℓ	$\left(\frac{1-mtr_y}{1-atr_y}\right) \sum_{\ell=1}^{n} \left(\frac{T_{i\ell}}{T_{v_i}}\right) e_{i\ell}$	no savings: $\gamma_i = 1$ For unit tax, t_u: replace v with $(t_u/p)/(1-t_u/p)$
2	As 1: with savings	As 1, mult by $(1 + \eta_{\gamma_i, z_i})$	$\gamma_i \neq 1; \eta_{\gamma_i, z_i} \neq 0$
3	As 1: $v_\ell' = v'$	$1 - \frac{t_k a_k'}{m_i} = \left(\frac{1-mtr_y}{1-atr_y}\right)$	$t_k a_k'$ = effective allowance
4	As 1: 2 rates	$\left(\frac{1-mtr_y}{1-atr_y}\right) \left[\frac{1-e^*}{1-w^*}\right]$	$v_\ell' = 0, \ \ell = 1, ..., s$ $v_\ell' = v', \ \ell > s$
	Combined Consumption and Income Tax: η_{R, y_i}		
	General	$\frac{T_v}{R} \eta_{T_v, y_i} + \left(1 - \frac{T_v}{R}\right) \eta_{T_y, y_i}$	
5	As 1	$\frac{mtr_y + \left\{(1-mtr_y)\sum_{\ell=1}^{n} v_\ell' w_{i\ell} e_{i\ell}\right\}}{atr_y + \left\{(1-atr_y)\sum_{\ell=1}^{n} v_\ell' w_{i\ell}\right\}}$	Excludes savings See (3.48)
6	As 2:	$1 + \frac{a_k'}{\Omega y_i - a_k'} = \frac{mtr_y + v'(1-mtr_y)}{atr_y + v'(1-atr_y)}$ $\Omega = \frac{1}{1-v'} + \left(\frac{v'}{1-v'}\right)\left(\frac{1-t_k}{t_k}\right)$	Uniform ad valorem rates
7	As 3:	$\frac{mtr_y + (1-mtr_y)v'(1-e^*)}{atr_y + (1-atr_y)v'(1-w^*)}$	

estimated are relatively limited, involving data on consumer budget shares for taxed goods in addition to tax parameters.

3.3 Changes in Consumption Tax Rates

This section examines the effect on the elasticities of changes in the indirect tax rates. The revenue elasticity for each income, y_i, in (3.18) is influenced by the budget shares, w_ℓ, and the income elasticities, e_ℓ, in addition to the income tax parameters, a'_k, t_k, appropriate to that income level and the consumption tax parameters consisting of the set of tax–inclusive rates $v'_\ell = v_\ell / (1 + v_\ell)$. The budget shares and total expenditure elasticities are also likely to vary with total expenditure, m_i. Any discretionary change in the consumption tax rates, designed perhaps to increase total tax revenue, therefore has a direct effect on the revenue elasticity in (3.18) and an indirect effect through endogenous changes in the budget shares.

Consider a change in prices arising from a change in indirect taxes. Given that the relationship between tax–inclusive and tax–exclusive prices, p_ℓ and $p_{E,\ell}$ respectively for good ℓ, is given by $p_\ell = (1 + v) p_{E,\ell}$, the proportionate change in the tax–inclusive price of the ℓth good, $\dot{p}_\ell$ resulting from a change in v_ℓ of dv_ℓ is given by:

$$\dot{p}_\ell = \frac{dv_\ell}{1 + v_\ell} \tag{3.49}$$

The proportionate change in the quantity consumed of good ℓ, $\dot{q}_\ell$, is given by:

$$\dot{q}_\ell = \sum_{r=1}^{n} e_{\ell r} \dot{p}_r \tag{3.50}$$

where $e_{\ell r}$ is the elasticity of demand for good ℓ with respect to a change in the price of the rth good, and $\dot{p}_r = dp_r / p_r$. The new expenditure on the ℓth good is given by $p_\ell q_\ell + d(p_\ell q_\ell)$ where the latter total differential is $p_\ell dq_\ell + q_\ell dp_\ell$ or $p_\ell q_\ell (\dot{q}_\ell + \dot{p}_\ell)$. Hence the proportional change in budget share of good ℓ resulting from a set of price changes is given by:

$$\dot{w}_\ell = \dot{p}_\ell + \sum_{r=1}^{n} e_{\ell r}\dot{p}_r \tag{3.51}$$

Since indirect tax revenue is given by $m_i \sum_{\ell=1}^{n} w_\ell v'_\ell$, the change in revenue resulting from a set of indirect tax changes is given by:

$$m_i \left\{ \sum_{\ell=1}^{n} \left(v'_\ell \frac{dw_\ell}{dv_\ell} + w_\ell \frac{dv'_\ell}{dv_\ell} \right) \right\}$$

and the proportional change in indirect tax revenue is therefore:

$$\frac{\sum_{\ell=1}^{n} w_\ell v'_\ell \left(\dot{w}_\ell + \dot{v}'_\ell \right)}{\sum_{\ell=1}^{n} w_\ell v'_\ell} \tag{3.52}$$

where $\dot{w}_\ell$ is obtained from (3.51). These results can be used to examine the effect of discretionary changes in taxation on total revenue and the revenue elasticity. However, the evaluation of such changes requires substantially more information than that of the revenue elasticities given above. In particular, information about the own–price and cross–price elasticities of demand is required for all goods, in order to compute the budget share changes, $\dot{w}_\ell$, associated with any change in consumption tax rates, and hence prices of goods.

3.4   The Aggregate Revenue Elasticity

As in the case of income taxes, the aggregate rather than the individual consumption tax elasticity is often more important for tax policy. For the equiproportional income growth case, aggregate consumption tax revenue elasticities can be obtained analogously to those given in chapter 2 for the multi–step income tax.

Let $T_V = \sum_{i=1}^{N} T_v(y_i)$ where, as earlier, $T_v(y_i) = m_i \sum_{\ell=1}^{n} v'_\ell w_\ell$.

Total differentiation gives:

$$dT_V = \sum_{i=1}^{N} \frac{\partial T_v(y_i)}{\partial y_i} dy_i$$

$$= \sum_{i=1}^{N} \eta_{T_v,y_i} T_v(y_i) \frac{dy_i}{y_i} \qquad (3.53)$$

For the equiproportional income growth case, substitute dY/Y for dy_i/y_i and divide by T_V to get:

$$\eta_{T_V,Y} = \sum_{i=1}^{N} \eta_{T_v,y_i} \frac{T_v(y_i)}{T_V} \qquad (3.54)$$

Thus, as in the case of the income tax, the aggregate consumption tax elasticity is a consumption–tax–share weighted average of the individual revenue elasticities.

The aggregate revenue elasticity, $\eta_{T_R,Y}$, including both income and consumption taxes is given, again in the equiproportional growth case, from (3.53) by:

$$\eta_{T_R,Y} = \sum_{i=1}^{N} \eta_{T_R,y_i} \left\{ \frac{T_y(y_i) + T_v(y_i)}{T_Y + T_V} \right\} \qquad (3.55)$$

and using (3.54) it can be found that (3.55) becomes:

$$\eta_{T_R,Y} = \left(\frac{T_Y}{T_Y + T_V} \right) \eta_{T_Y,Y} + \left(\frac{T_V}{T_Y + T_V} \right) \eta_{T_V,Y} \qquad (3.56)$$

Hence the aggregate revenue elasticity is simply a revenue–share weighted average of the aggregate income tax and consumption tax elasticities.

3.5 Illustrative Examples

Section 3.2 demonstrated that both income and consumption tax revenue elasticities can be calculated, for the individual taxpayer, from information on relatively few parameters. These include income tax rates, t_k, the effective allowance, a'_k, and indirect tax rates, v_ℓ, together with the budget shares and expenditure elasticities for goods bearing different tax rates. With the restriction of equiproportionate income growth, equivalent aggregate expressions were also shown to be tractable. These require information about the income distribution in order to calculate revenue weights; see (3.53) and (3.54)). How non–equiproportionate income growth may be handled in practice is discussed in chapters 5 and 7.

This section provides illustrations of the alternative revenue elasticities. The tax parameters used are based on a stylised version of the Australian income and consumption tax system before and after the replacement of a set of excises with a more uniform *ad valorem* Goods and Service Tax (GST) in 2000. After various alternative rate combinations were considered, a GST at 10 per cent (with some exemptions) was eventually introduced. The income tax schedule involves four rates and thresholds; those used for illustration approximate the schedule in the mid–1990s. The thresholds are 6000, 21000, 38000, and 50000 (A\$), and marginal income tax rates applied to taxable income above these thresholds, t_k, are 0.20, 0.355, 0.44 and 0.47 respectively.

Total expenditure elasticities are required for each expenditure category facing a different tax rate. Individual values cannot of course be observed, so they must be based on some type of grouping of individuals using a sample survey. These were obtained using the 1993 Australian Household Expenditure Survey (HES); the method is described in more detail in chapter 6. Essentially this involves identifying the budget shares for the 14 expenditure categories used by the HES across 30 household total expenditure groups. The 14 groups are those for which different effective *ad valorem* tax rates have been estimated for the pre–GST excise regime, as shown in Table 3.2. Estimating changes in budget shares across those expenditure groups then allows expenditure elasticities to be obtained as shown by (3.11). The results of this exercise revealed that, in the Australian case, budget shares fall over most of the relevant range of total expenditure in the cases of: current housing costs; electricity, gas and other fuels; food and non–alcoholic beverages; postal and telephone charges, health services; and personal care products.

Alternatively, the shares rise as income rises in the case of: clothing and footwear; furniture and appliances; motor vehicles and parts; recreational items; miscellaneous; and house building payments. In the cases of alcohol and tobacco the budget shares initially rise before falling in the higher–income groups.

Consumption tax calculations illustrate three alternative tax regimes, shown in Table 3.2. The column headed (i) shows the highly variable effective consumption tax rates arising from the complex range of indirect taxes operating in Australia prior to the GST. These rates are estimated on the assumption that the taxes are fully shifted forward, using the method devised by Scutella (1997) which makes use of the matrix of inter–industry transactions. This system of highly variable rates is compared with two simpler cases, shown in columns (ii) and (iii). Column (ii) is a uniform 15 per cent *ad valorum* rate, while column (iii) is similar to (ii) but with three zero–rated categories: current housing costs, house building costs, and food and beverages. In countries using value added consumption taxes, these categories are commonly zero–rated.

3.5.1 Individual Revenue Elasticities

Using the data decsribed above, this subsection illustrates the properties of individual elasticities, based on the simplest, uniform consumption tax case. Using the income tax expression (3.4) and the consumption tax expression (3.28), elasticities may be calculated for alternative income levels. The income tax case illustrated adopts the assumption $\eta_{a'_k, y_i} = 0$, which is appropriate in this case. Illustrative results are shown in Table 3.3. More details of the variation in the elasticities with income are given in Figure 3.1. This figure shows the tendency for the income tax elasticity to decline within each marginal rate band, with step increases as thresholds are crossed.

Table 3.2: Indirect Tax Rates

no.	Commodity Group	Tax Structure		
		(i)	(ii)	(iii)
1	Current housing costs	0.1437	0.15	0.00
2	Electricity, gas and other fuels	0.0956	0.15	0.15
3	Food and beverages	0.1289	0.15	0.00
4	Spirits, beer and wine	0.4224	0.15	0.15
5	Tobacco	2.1510	0.15	0.15
6	Clothing and footwear	0.0731	0.15	0.15
7	Furniture and appliances	0.1201	0.15	0.15
8	Postal and telephone charges	0.0993	0.15	0.15
9	Health services	0.0603	0.15	0.15
10	Motor vehicles and parts	0.3126	0.15	0.15
11	Recreational items	0.1677	0.15	0.15
12	Personal care products	0.1441	0.15	0.15
13	Miscellaneous	0.1644	0.15	0.15
14	House building payments	0.1296	0.15	0.00

The reverse occurs for consumption taxes, as may be expected from (3.28): the elasticity increases within income tax bands with step decreases across thresholds. Table 3.3 also highlights the tendency (at least for income levels at the mid–point within tax bands) for the income tax elasticity to decline but for the consumption tax elasticity to decline initially and then increase at high income levels. This consumption tax phenomenon (which is also characteristic of aggregate consumption tax elasticities – see below), arises here because the increase in mtr_y in (3.28) as a result of crossing into higher marginal tax bands (and which reduces the consumption tax elasticity) is reversed as incomes increase beyond each threshold when mtr_y is constant but atr_y continues to rise, thus increasing the consumption tax elasticity. As is evident from (3.28) however, the consumption tax elasticity cannot exceed unity (for this uniform consumption tax rate case).

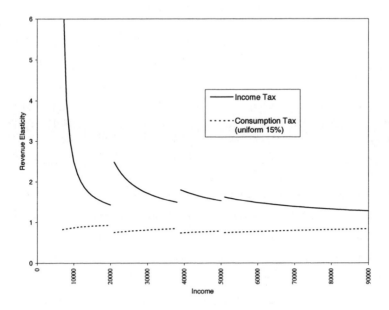

Figure 3.1: Individual Income and Consumption Tax Elasticities

3.5.2 Aggregate Revenue Elasticities

The calculation of aggregate revenue elasticities is based on the use of a random sample of 10,000 individuals from a lognormal income distribution having a variance of logarithms of 0.5; this is obviously a simplification but, for present purposes, provides a reasonable approximation of the Australian income distribution. The simulated population is initially obtained using a specified mean of logarithms, and equiproportionate growth of the 10,000 pre–tax incomes is then imposed over the relevant range. The individual income tax revenue elasticities used to calculate the aggregate equivalents were obtained simply by calculating the average and marginal tax rates facing each individual, since the elasticity is the ratio of the former to the latter.

Table 3.3: Individual Revenue Elasticities: Uniform Taxes

			Income Tax Band			
	0-6000	6001-21000	21001-38000	38001-50000	50001+	
t_k	0	0.2	0.355	0.44	0.47	0.47
a'_k	0	6000	12560	17380	19560	19560
y_i	3000	13500	29500	44000	75000	150000
m_i	3000	12000	23480	32290	48900	88700
η_{T_y,y_i}	0	1.80	1.74	1.65	1.35	1.15
η_{T_v,y_i}	0	0.90	0.81	0.76	0.81	0.89

This avoids the need to calculate a'_k for each individual and tax schedule. Resulting profiles for the income tax, consumption tax and total tax revenue elasticities are shown in Figure 3.2 for the multiple consumption tax rate case in column (i) of Table 3.2. Figure 3.3 compares consumption tax elasticity profiles for the three cases listed in Table 3.2.

The aggregate elasticities in Figure 3.2 display a similar pattern to the individual revenue elasticities shown in Figure 3.1: income tax revenue is elastic but declining, while consumption tax revenue is inelastic and relatively constant. As average income doubles from around A$17,000 to A$34,000 the income tax elasticity declines from around 1.75 to 1.5, while the consumption tax elasticity declines slightly from 0.88 to 0.82. The effect on the total tax revenue elasticity is to produce a relatively flat schedule with the elasticity within the 1.2–1.4 range over a wide range of mean income levels.

Comparing the consumption tax elasticity profiles shown in Figure 3.3, profile B, the uniform rate case, is the aggregate equivalent of the individual elasticity profile in Figure 3.1 and displays a similar pattern, rising for mean incomes above about A$35,000 for the reasons outlined earlier. Introducing exemptions, as in profile C, increases the elasticity at all income levels, as predicted for the two–rate case above. However, increases are greatest at lower income levels and the profile is almost flat at high average incomes. This difference from profile B reflects the fact that two of the zero–rated categories

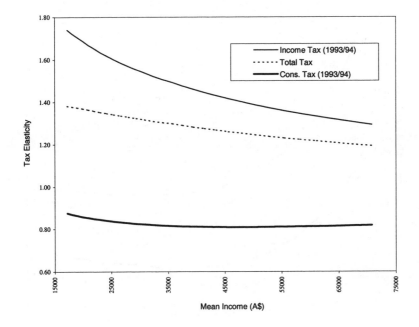

Figure 3.2: Aggregate Income and Consumption Tax Elasticities

have expenditure elasticities less than unity, and hence falling budget shares. This element of progressivity serves to increase the consumption tax revenue elasticity, especially at low mean incomes.

Profile A, for the multiple tax rates observed in Australia before the introduction of the GST, reveals intermediate elasticity levels at lower mean income levels compared with the other two cases, but has the lowest elasticity at high incomes. As mentioned earlier, unlike the uniform case B, both cases A and C could, in principle, produce consumption tax elasticities in excess of unity. However, in these particular cases any progressivity arising from the consumption tax exemptions, or differential rates, is insufficient to outweigh the inelastic effect arising from the progressive income tax. Simulating the

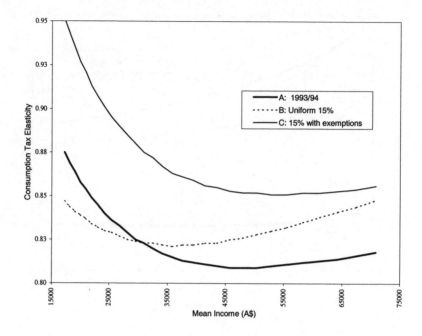

Figure 3.3: Aggregate Consumption Tax Elasticities

case in which the four main categories with expenditure elasticities less than unity (categories 1, 2, 3, and 9 in Table 3.2) are zero–rated, with all other goods at 15 per cent, is found to yield consumption tax revenue elasticities slightly above unity.

3.6   Conclusions

This chapter has shown that tractable analytical expressions can be produced for the built–in flexibility, or revenue elasticities, of various indirect taxes and for combined direct–plus–indirect taxes, where the indirect tax system is combined with a general multi–step income tax structure. These results clarify the determinants of the revenue responsiveness properties of different taxes, and demonstrate that indirect tax elasticities can be estimated from information that is generally available for most tax systems: summary tax parameters and total expenditure elasticities for commodity groups.

Two simple, but useful, results to emerge from the analysis are as follows. First, in a uniform consumption tax rate system, consumption tax revenue must be income–inelastic provided the income tax system is progressive. The elasticity of total income–plus–consumption taxes, however, must exceed unity. Second, for the more common two–rate or multi–rate cases, whether or not consumption tax revenue is elastic is ambiguous but depends on two simple conditions: whether the income tax is regressive or progressive, and the average expenditure elasticity of zero–rated (lower–rated) goods. Consumption taxes are more likely to be elastic if income taxes are regressive and if zero–rated goods are mainly necessities. In practice, while the latter condition often holds, the former does not, so that consumption taxes are expected typically to display inelastic revenue properties. The effects of changes in indirect tax rates on revenue elasticities were also examined analytically, showing that to estimate these in practice requires more information, particularly relating to price elasticities of demand.

Applying the built–in flexibility expressions to illustrative tax data and expenditure elasticity estimates, based on a stylised version of the Australian tax system, income and consumption tax revenue elasticities were calculated for a simulated income distribution. These confirmed the tractability of the analytical expressions and demonstrated the inelasticity of consumption taxes, both absolutely and relative to income tax elasticities. While it is possible for consumption tax revenue elasticities slightly to exceed unity, in practice this would appear to require low or zero rates on a substantial proportion of consumption expenditure, concentrated on those goods which form large budget shares at low income levels.

The various tax parameters in the elasticity expressions obtained here also highlight the potential impact of tax reform on built–in flexibility. When governments make discretionary changes to tax parameters, such as tax rates and allowances, the direct effect on tax revenue is of immediate concern both to the treasury and to the taxpayers. However, the effects of such changes on the built–in flexibility of individual taxes or the tax system as a whole are often less well appreciated. Year–to–year changes will generally have small impacts on revenue elasticities, but these can build up to more substantial effects over longer periods, especially when compounded by subsequent reforms. For example, from the early 1980s a number of industrialised countries undertook significant tax reform, often involving a shift towards a less progressive income tax and greater use of indirect taxes, as well as experiencing rising mean incomes relative to tax thresholds, and increased inequality of pre–tax incomes. Each of these changes can be expected to affect tax revenue elasticities, with important implications for future automatic revenue growth. These aspects are examined in more detail for specific countries in the empirical applications in Part III.

Chapter 4

Tax Revenue and Labour Supply

Previous chapters on the built–in flexibility of taxation have concentrated on the analysis of tax revenue elasticities with respect to income growth at the individual and aggregate levels. However, where it is desired to consider the effects on revenue growth of growth in the economy arising, for example, from productivity growth, the relationship between tax revenue and wage rate growth is more relevant. In this case, elasticities with respect to income or earnings provide only part of the story. Changes in wage rates and gross incomes may be quite different, especially in the neighbourhood of income thresholds in piecewise–linear tax structures. This can be important for projecting revenue growth in practice.

In the UK, for example, the Treasury projects income growth forward based on projections of average income levels and employment. Over the long–run, average income is assumed to grow at the economy's long–run rate of productivity growth, of approximately 2.5 per cent, plus the expected inflation rate, with judgemental adjustments in the short–run as the economy moves to or from its long–run trend. There is therefore no allowance for labour supply effects and if real wage rate growth approximates productivity growth, this is also be the assumed rate of average income growth.

The present chapter explores the income tax revenue responsiveness arising from wage rate changes when labour supply is endogenous. It shows how analytical expressions can be extended to incorporate these endogenous labour supply responses. Numerical examples are constructed to examine revenue elasticities in the face of highly nonlinear tax structures. A feature of such structures is that multiple local optima may exist and large discrete jumps in labour supply can arise from non–convex ranges of budget sets. An objective is to identify how far, and in what circumstances, labour supply effects can alter the revenue responsiveness estimates that are typically computed, both for individual taxpayers and in aggregate.

Section 4.1 shows how the revenue elasticities with respect to income and wages are related to each other and to labour supply elasticities at the individual level. The elasticity of revenue with respect to the wage rate depends on both the revenue elasticity with respect to income and the elasticity of income with respect to the wage. Furthermore, the latter is a function of the elasticity of hours worked with respect to the wage rate. When the tax–wage relationship is of interest, it is therefore necessary to consider how a change in wages affects labour–leisure choices, given the existing tax schedule. To the extent that there is any automatic indexation of tax thresholds, these are usually in relation to income, rather than wage changes. Section 4.2 provides an indication of potential orders of magnitude. Section 4.3 turns to aggregate revenue elasticities and provides numerical examples. Brief conclusions are in section 4.4.

4.1   Tax Revenue Elasticities

To see how endogenous labour supply affects tax revenue elasticities with respect to wage rate changes, it is helpful to begin with some basic relationships among various elasticities at the individual level. These are examined in subsection 4.1.1. Comparisons with standard built–in flexibility results for income taxation, in the context of a multi–step function, are then provided in subsection 4.1.2.

4.1.1 Basic Relationships

Consider an individual who has a gross wage rate, w, and supplies h hours of labour, resulting in a gross income of $y = wh$. The tax paid is:

$$T(y) = T(y(w)) \qquad (4.1)$$

The standard tax revenue elasticity, denoted $\eta_{T,y}$ and referred to here as the 'tax–income elasticity' is given by:

$$\eta_{T,y} = \frac{y}{T(y)}\frac{dT(y)}{dy} = \frac{mtr}{atr} \qquad (4.2)$$

where mtr and atr are the marginal and average rates respectively. The elasticity of $T(y)$ with respect to the wage rate, denoted $\eta_{T,w}$ and referred to as the 'tax–wage elasticity', can be expressed as:

$$\eta_{T,w} = \eta_{T,y}\eta_{y,w} \qquad (4.3)$$

Furthermore, using $y = wh$, the elasticity of earnings with respect to the wage, $\eta_{y,w}$, can be written as:

$$\eta_{y,w} = 1 + \eta_{h,w} \qquad (4.4)$$

giving:

$$\eta_{T,w} = \eta_{T,y}(1 + \eta_{h,w}) \qquad (4.5)$$

Although $\eta_{T,y}$ is endogenous, it is useful to express (4.5) in this way because $\eta_{T,y}$ is typically estimated from data on incomes and tax revenues. Thus, together with estimates of $\eta_{h,w}$, the tax–wage elasticity may be obtained.

4.1.2   Income Tax Revenue

Most income tax structures take the form of a multi–step function with K gross income thresholds, a_k, and effective marginal tax rates applying above those thresholds, t_k, for $k = 1, ..., K$. It was shown in chapter 2 that for such a function, the tax revenue, $T(y)$, can be written, for an individual on the kth linear segment, as:

$$T(y) = t_k (y - a_k') \tag{4.6}$$

with:

$$a_k' = \sum_{j=2}^{k} a_j \left\{ \frac{(t_j - t_{j-1})}{t_k} \right\} \tag{4.7}$$

From (4.6), marginal and average income tax rates are $mtr = t_k$ and $atr = t_k - (a_k' t_k / y)$, so that the elasticity of income tax with respect to income is, from (4.2):

$$\eta_{T,y} = \frac{y}{y - a_k'} \tag{4.8}$$

Equation (4.8) is the simplest income tax revenue elasticity, derived in chapter 2, for the exogenous labour supply case where the tax thresholds a_k are fixed. (This may at first sight suggest that the elasticity does not depend on the tax rates, but the threshold a_k' depends on the rate structure.) However, in many income tax systems, a number of deductions are income related so that $da_k'/dy > 0$. Allowing for this possibility, and defining $\eta_{a_k',y}$ as the elasticity of allowances with respect to income, chapter 2 showed that (4.8) becomes:

$$\eta_{T,y} = \frac{y - a_k' \eta_{a_k',y}}{y - a_k'} \tag{4.9}$$

A corresponding elasticity of allowances with respect to the wage rate can be written as:

$$\eta_{a_k',w} = \eta_{a_k',y} \eta_{y,w} \tag{4.10}$$

Hence:

$$\eta_{a_k',y} = \frac{\eta_{a_k',w}}{1 + \eta_{h,w}} \tag{4.11}$$

Table 4.1: Examples of Elasticities

$\eta_{h,w}$	$\eta_{a_k',w}$	$\eta_{T,w}$
0.05	0.2625	1.3970
0.10	0.2750	1.4636
0.15	0.2875	1.5301
0.20	0.3000	1.5966
0.25	0.3125	1.6631

Substituting (4.11) into (4.9) gives:

$$\eta_{T,y} = \frac{y(1 + \eta_{h,w}) - a_k' \eta_{a_k',w}}{(y - a_k')(1 + \eta_{h,w})} \qquad (4.12)$$

and using (4.5):

$$\eta_{T,w} = \frac{y(1 + \eta_{h,w}) - a_k' \eta_{a_k',w}}{(y - a_k')} \qquad (4.13)$$

These expressions show how the tax–wage, and tax–income, elasticities can both be decomposed into components associated with the labour supply elasticity, $\eta_{h,w}$, and the elasticity of income tax allowances with respect to wages, $\eta_{a_k',w}$.

To illustrate possible values, consider an individual earning gross income of $y = £17,000$ per year, with $a_k' = 5200$ and $\eta_{a_k',y} = 0.25$. These values approximate those corresponding to average income and the tax structure in the UK in the late 1990s. Such an individual would be paying a marginal tax rate of $t = 0.23$, but this does not influence the examples below, since they apply for assumed values of the labour supply elasticity. Table 4.1 provides examples of potential orders of magnitude for several assumed labour supply elasticities, $\eta_{h,w}$. In each case, $\eta_{T,y} = 1.3305$: this elasticity is constant for given values of y, a_k', and $\eta_{a_k',y}$, as seen from (4.9).

Empirical estimates available for the UK generally find small positive labour supply elasticities for men, within the range used in Table 4.1; see, for example, Blundell and Walker (1982) and Blundell *et al.* (1998). Blundell and MaCurdy (1999) provide a review of empirical estimates. Disney and

Smith (2002) find more substantial hours responses by pensionable men in the UK; and Bingley and Lanot (2002) find a labour supply elasticity around 0.14 for a sample of Danish private sector workers. However, potentially larger effects on revenue elasticities are to be expected for individuals close to tax thresholds and for aggregate revenue elasticities where a sufficiently large proportion of the wage distribution is affected by these thresholds. The following section explores individual effects further by modelling labour supply responses explicitly in the context of a means–tested transfer payment combined with income taxation.

4.2 Modelling Individual Elasticities

This section provides a detailed examination of individual elasticities using a simple tax and transfer system. In practice, tax and transfer systems display considerable complexity. However, to illustrate the wide range of possible labour supply responses and resulting tax revenue elasticities it is sufficient to analyse a simple tax and transfer system: this is described in subsection 4.2.1. The labour supply behaviour arising from this system is considered in subsection 4.2.2. Individual income tax revenue elasticities and benefit elasticities are examined in subsections 4.2.3 and 4.2.4 respectively.

4.2.1 A Tax and Transfer System

In modelling income tax revenue elasticities with respect to wages, it is not sufficient to consider the income tax structure alone, since labour supply modelling requires the full tax and benefit system, which determines individuals' budget sets, to be specified. Any piecewise–linear tax and transfer system can be specified by a number of effective marginal tax rates and gross earnings values at which the marginal rates change. Attention is restricted here to the case where earnings from employment and transfer payments are the only sources of income, and tax thresholds are fixed such that $\eta_{a'_k,y} = 0$.

Suppose there is an income tax involving four marginal tax rates, $t_1, ..., t_4$, and income thresholds, $a_1, ..., a_4$. Let $t_1 = a_1 = 0$, so there is a tax–free threshold of a_2. The income tax is combined with a means–tested transfer system in which non–workers receive a benefit of b. The benefit is gradually withdrawn as income rises above zero, but for those who are eligible, net income, z, is given by:

$$z = b + (1 - s) y \qquad (4.14)$$

Hence the effective marginal rate for recipients is s. Those with $a_2 > y > 0$, who work but face a marginal income tax rate of zero, receive a benefit equal to $b - sy$.

Those with earnings in the range $a_3 > y > a_2$ pay income tax, so that their after–income–tax income is $a_2 + (1 - t_2)(y - a_2) = t_2 a_2 + (1 - t_2) y$. If this is less than the corresponding net income given by (4.14), they receive a transfer to bring them up to the appropriate level. The social transfer received by such individuals is equal to $b + (1 - s) y - t_2 a_2 + (1 - t_2) y$, which can be simplified to $b - t_2 a_2 - y(s - t_2)$. This transfer payment becomes zero at the income level y', given by:

$$y' = \frac{b - t_2 a_2}{s - t_2} \qquad (4.15)$$

Hence y' is an effective income threshold for the combined tax/transfer system. Only those with $y < y'$ receive any benefits and are subject to the effective overall marginal tax rate of s. Those with $a_3 > y > y'$ pay income tax at the marginal rate t_2 and receive no transfer payments. The combined system therefore has effective marginal rates of s, t_2, t_3 and t_4 applying above thresholds of $a_1 = 0$, y', a_3 and a_4. This ensures that the overall tax structure has no discontinuities. The relationship between gross and net income is shown in Figure 4.1.

Suppose $s = 0.5$ and $b = 60$, expressed in weekly terms. Let $a_2 = 80$ and $t_2 = 0.10$. Substituting into (4.15) gives an earnings threshold of $y' = 130$ per week, above which the marginal tax rate is 0.10 and below which it is

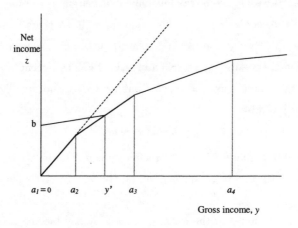

Figure 4.1: The Relationship Between Gross and Net Income

Table 4.2: A Hypothetical Tax Structure

Income Tax		Tax/Transfer	
Threshold	MTR	Threshold	EMTR
0	0	0	0.50
80	0.10	130	0.10
180	0.23	180	0.23
600	0.40	600	0.40

0.5. Further detail of the hypothetical structure used below is given in Table 4.2, where the effective overall structure is given on the right–hand side of the table. These values in Table 4.2 (suitably annualised) approximate the UK income tax structure around the year 2000.

4.2.2   Labour Supply

The effective tax structure shown on the right–hand side of Table 4.2 has a range where the implied budget set for each individual is non–convex, giving rise to a large discrete jump in labour supply at a particular 'switching' wage. A diagrammatic exposition of labour supply with such nonlinear budget sets is given in Appendix 4.1. The switches occur where the individual's indifference curve is simultaneously tangential to two segments, or simultaneously touches one corner and a segment, or two corners. This switching wage is lower than the value associated with the earnings threshold of y'; indeed, the non–convexity implies that earnings in a range around y' would not be observed.

The labour supply curve can be generated numerically using an explicit assumption about preferences. Suppose utility functions take the Cobb–Douglas form. This is chosen merely for convenience of presentation in order to illustrate the basic properties of the models; similar results were obtained for constant elasticity of substitution (CES) utility functions. However, care must be taken when using the CES form, since supply curves relating to linear segments of the budget constraint can be 'backward bending' if the elasticity of substitution between leisure and net income is less than unity. Furthermore, the choice of coefficients on leisure and consumption are no longer independent of the units.

With Cobb–Douglas preferences, consumption (net income) of z and time spent in work of h, from a total of H available hours, utility is:

$$U(c,h) = z^\alpha (H-h)^{1-\alpha} \tag{4.16}$$

A piecewise–linear budget constraint is made up of series of segments. The kth segment is defined by its virtual income (the intercept where $h = 0$) of m_k and effective marginal tax rate of t_k. The hours range for which the segment applies are also required. To construct the budget constraint it is thus necessary to convert the various income thresholds and rates used in the tax structure into hours ranges, for a given wage rate, and to obtain the required virtual incomes. The transformation is described in Appendix 4.2. Full income, M, that is, income after the endowment of H hours is converted to money at the appropriate net wage of $w\left(1-t_k\right)$, is given by:

$$M = w(1 - t_k)H + m_k \qquad (4.17)$$

Maximisation of (4.16) subject to (4.17) gives the standard Cobb–Douglas result for the demand for leisure:

$$H - h = (1 - \alpha)\frac{M}{w\left(1 - t_k\right)} \qquad (4.18)$$

Hence labour supply is:

$$h = \alpha H - \frac{m_k\left(1 - \alpha\right)}{w\left(1 - t_k\right)} \qquad (4.19)$$

The value of h is jointly determined along with the segment, giving the values of m_k and t_k, or the relevant corner of the budget constraint. As the budget set has non–convex ranges where the marginal tax rate declines, determination of the optimal solution is complicated by the possibility of more than one local optimum and the existence of a threshold wage rate at which the individual makes a large discrete jump from one section of the budget constraint to another. However, if marginal rates always increase, there is only one local optimum. An efficient algorithm is used below to search over all segments and corner solutions to determine the optimal labour supply. For a description of the algorithm used, which allows for the possibility of multiple local optima where non–convexities exist, see Creedy and Duncan (2002).

The potential importance of labour supply effects for revenue elasticities can be seen from the labour supply curve in Figure 4.2, which applies to an individual with $\alpha = 0.5$. This reveals a number of kinks and segments associated with the various tax and benefit thresholds and the switching wage where a jump is made from the first to the second segment. The individual does not begin working until the wage of $w = 1.52$ is reached. Below this wage rate, the full benefit of 60 is obtained. As soon as the individual starts to

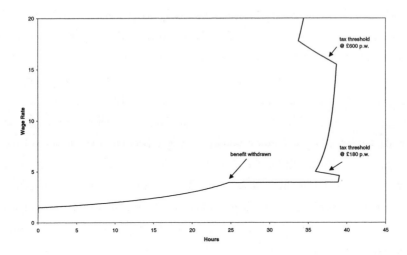

Figure 4.2: Individual Labour Supply Curve

work, the effective marginal tax rate of 0.5 applies up to the income threshold of 130.

For a wage rate above 3.52 the individual begins to pay income tax and simultaneously receives a benefit. Labour supply is therefore relatively elastic over this range. The wage of approximately 3.96 is found to be the switching wage associated with a substantial jump in hours worked (from 25 to 39 hours). This involves a jump to the next segment of the budget constraint, so that the individual no longer receives any benefit and there is a consequent drop in the effective marginal tax rate (from 0.5 to 0.1).

Above the switching wage, labour supply is relatively inelastic, except for backward–bending segments associated with kinks in the budget constraint (where marginal rates rise) at the two highest income tax thresholds of $y = 180$ and 600. At these kink points, $\eta_{h,w} = -1$ so that $\eta_{y,w} = 0$ over the range of wage rates for which the kinks are optimal. Gross earnings remain constant at the relevant income threshold as the wage rate increases, with each of these backward-bending labour supply curve segments forming part of rectangular hyperbolas. The profile of elasticities as the wage rate increases is shown in Figure 4.3. This has high elasticities at the wage where the individual begins to supply labour and where there is a discrete jump between segments of the budget constrait. These high elasticities, as well as the ranges where the elasticity is -1, are associated with the piecewise–linear budget constraint, and would be expected irrespective of the nature of the utility function chosen for the illustration. Elasticities in the other sections of the profile are within the sort of range observed in practice, although direct comparisons are difficult because empirical studies do not report such variations, but concentrate on, for example, values at average wages. From equation (4.19) it is readily shown that:

$$\eta_{h,w} = \frac{\alpha(1-t)wH}{t(1-\alpha)a} - 1 \qquad (4.20)$$

so that, for a given tax structure and wage rate, the labour supply elasticity is directly related to α. Although the Cobb–Douglas form is not used in applied work, it is suitable for the present illustrations, yielding plausible elasticity values. As is shown below, with even a simple tax and transfer system, it is the associated kinks and nonconvexities in the budget constraint that primarily determine labour supply elasticities, with α affecting the wage rates at which these kinks and discontinuities occur.

4.2.3 Revenue Elasticities

Figures 4.4 and 4.5 show the associated revenue elasticity profiles. The elasticities were computed by increasing w by a small amount, 2 per cent, at each step, and recalculating optimal labour supply and taxation. In Figure 4.4, $\eta_{T,w}$ is compared with the equivalent profile for the case where labour supply is exogenous. The zero labour supply case is obtained by setting the exogenous level of hours worked at the maximum level chosen in the endogenous

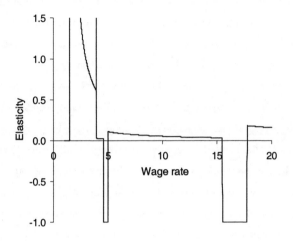

Figure 4.3: Labour Supply Elasticities

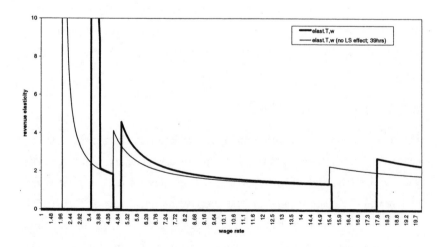

Figure 4.4: Tax–Wage Elasticities

case (that is, 39 hours per week). Figure 4.4 reveals that ignoring endogenous labour supply responses leads to $\eta_{T,w}$ being underestimated except at corner solutions where $\eta_{T,w} = 0$ in the endogenous case, but the exogenous case leads to positive values. This occurs, particularly at low wage levels, because the lower gross earnings associated with responses to the tax–benefit system are ignored in the exogenous case. With such differences between the two profiles, especially at wages below around £5 per hour, it is unclear how aggregate elasticities based on a wage distribution might be affected.

Figure 4.5 compares $\eta_{T,w}$ with $\eta_{T,y}$ for the endogenous labour supply case. This shows that, given endogenous labour supply, $\eta_{T,y}$ can be expected to be less than $\eta_{T,w}$ at all wage rates except at corners where both $\eta_{T,w}$ and $\eta_{T,y}$ are zero. Both elasticities can be very large for individuals immediately above tax thresholds. However, it can be seen that positively valued elasticities are generally in the range of 1 to 3.

Figure 4.6 shows the ratio of the tax–wage and tax–income elasticities, providing an indication of the extent of underestimation at different wage levels if $\eta_{T,y}$ is used as a proxy for $\eta_{T,w}$. Apart from low wage levels, where $\eta_{T,w}$ can exceed $\eta_{T,y}$ by as much as 70–80 per cent, for most wage rates $\eta_{T,w}$ exceeds $\eta_{T,y}$ by less than 20 per cent, and more typically by less than 10 per cent.

4.2.4 Benefit Elasticities

Figure 4.7 provides information about the variation in the benefit elasticity, that is, the responsiveness of transfer expenditures to changes in wage rates. This is negative, reflecting the withdrawal of benefits as wages rates rise, and values obviously depend on the effective marginal rate applied (0.5 in this case). The elasticity changes from around −0.5, when the benefit taper begins to apply, to around −3.5 when income tax becomes payable. This temporarily increases the benefit elasticity which continues to fall thereafter

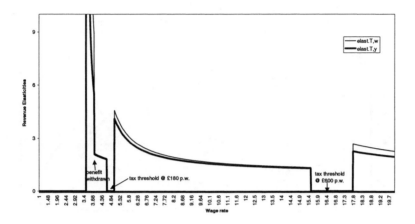

Figure 4.5: Tax-Income and Tax-Wage Elasticities

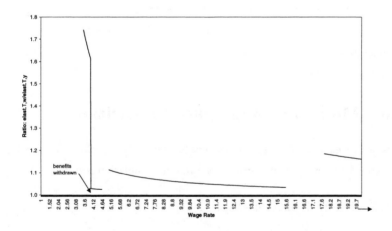

Figure 4.6: Elasticity Ratio

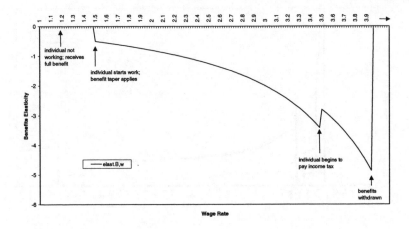

Figure 4.7: Individual Benefit Elasticity

until benefits are completely withdrawn (at the point where the individual jumps to the next segment of the budget constraint). These values suggest that, even with a fairly modest taper rate of 0.5, the benefit elasticity can be large in absolute value, causing transfer expenditures to decline relatively quickly as wage rates rise.

4.3   Modelling Aggregate Elasticities

This section examines aggregate revenue elasticities. Subsection 4.3.1 presents the basic formulae and subsection 4.3.2 reports simulation results.

4.3.1   Basic Relationships

For a continuous wage rate distribution, where the distribution function is $F(w)$, total tax revenue, T_Y, can be expressed as:

$$T_Y = \int T\left(y\left(w\right)\right) dF\left(w\right) \tag{4.21}$$

The elasticity of aggregate revenue, with respect to a change in the arithmetic mean wage, W, can be written as:

$$\eta_{T_Y,W} = \int \eta_{T,w} \eta_{w,W} \frac{T(y(w))}{T_Y} dF(w) \qquad (4.22)$$

where $\eta_{w,W}$ is the elasticity of w with respect to the average wage. In the equiproportional case where all wage rates change in equal proportions, $\eta_{w,W} = 1$ and the aggregate elasticity is the tax–share weighted average of individual elasticities:

$$\eta_{T_Y,W} = \int \eta_{T,y} \eta_{y,w} \frac{T(y(w))}{T_Y} dF(w) \qquad (4.23)$$

The further analysis of equation (4.23) must allow for the number of different linear segments in the tax function, each having a different m_k and t_k, and the wage thresholds over which each combination is applicable. As mentioned above, for those who are in ranges of w that place them at corners, small changes in w have no effect on y, so $\eta_{y,w} = 0$ over that range. In general it would be extremely complex to derive the precise thresholds since, for example, the switching wage cannot be obtained explicitly except for very simple cases. For further analysis of switching wage rates, using Cobb–Douglas utilities and a simple means–tested benefit system, see Creedy (1996). For this reason, simulation methods are used in this section where revenue elasticities are based on a random sample of individuals drawn from a specified wage rate distribution.

4.3.2 Simulation Results

Simulation of the aggregate tax revenue elasticity requires a form for the wage distribution. The following examples are based on the use of a lognormal distribution, $\Lambda(\mu, \sigma^2)$, where μ and σ^2 are respectively the mean and variance of the logarithms of hourly wage rates. Values of $\mu = 2.0$ and $\sigma^2 = 0.5$ were chosen, giving a mean hourly wage rate of $\exp(\mu + \frac{1}{2}\sigma^2) = 9.49$. Results are reported for a random sample of 5000 individuals drawn from this distribution. As before, each individual elasticity was obtained by increasing the wage by 2 per cent and recalculating the labour supply, income and tax variables. Simulations excluded the small number of individuals for whom the small wage increase led to a large discrete jump in labour supply from the first to the second segment of the budget constraint, or a move from a corner to a tangency solutions. Elasticities for these individuals are disproportionately large. For convenience, simulations assume a common value of the preference parameter, α, across all individuals, though in practice this may vary if, for example, high wages are associated with a lower leisure preference. Creedy (2001) discusses the appropriate simulation method for the case where w and α are jointly lognormally distributed.

Table 4.3 shows values of both $\eta_{T_Y,W}$ and $\eta_{T_Y,Y}$ for a range of values of α, together with the ratio, $\eta_{T_Y,W}/\eta_{T_Y,Y}$. For example, with $\alpha = 0.5$, column 4 indicates that the aggregate tax–wage elasticity is approximately 9 per cent greater than the tax–income elasticity. However, the ratio of elasticities does not show directly the difference in tax revenue growth associated with the two elasticity measures, though expected revenue growth is a key variable for forecasters. The measure in column 5 is the ratio of the proportionate change in tax revenues predicted by the two tax elasticities, and is given by $\left(\eta_{T,W} - 1\right)/\left(\eta_{T,Y} - 1\right)$. This shows the extent to which revenue growth is underestimated if $\eta_{T_Y,W}$ is used as a proxy for $\eta_{T_Y,Y}$. Column 5 shows that, with $\alpha = 0.5$ for example, the proportionate increase in tax revenue using $\eta_{T_Y,W}$, $(\eta_{T_Y,W} - 1 = 0.636)$ is around 27 per cent greater $(0.636/0.502)$ than would be obtained using $\eta_{T_Y,Y}$ $(\eta_{T_Y,Y} - 1 = 0.502)$. However, as α approaches unity, the labour supply effects are reduced and the elasticities become closer. These differences between $\eta_{T_Y,W}$ and $\eta_{T_Y,Y}$ do not primarily arise because an individual's labour supply elasticity (such as those shown in Figure 4.2) is sensitive to the value of α, but rather because of differing degrees of bunching by individuals around kinks and discontinuities, for differing leisure preferences, α.

Table 4.3: Aggregate Elasticities

α	$\eta_{T_Y,W}$	$\eta_{T_Y,Y}$	$\dfrac{\eta_{T_Y,W}}{\eta_{T_Y,Y}}$	$\dfrac{\eta_{T_Y,W}-1}{\eta_{T_Y,Y}-1}$
0.1	2.095	1.844	1.14	1.31
0.3	1.776	1.597	1.11	1.30
0.5	1.636	1.502	1.09	1.27
0.7	1.544	1.463	1.06	1.18
0.9	1.468	1.442	1.02	1.06

Table 4.4: Wage Thresholds: Alternative Preference Parameters

	Wage Threshold		
Description	$\alpha = 0.3$	$\alpha = 0.5$	$\alpha = 0.7$
Start work	3.52	1.52	0.66
Pay income tax $y = 80$	6.84	3.52	2.08
Jump over $y = 130$	7.08	3.96	2.62
Reach corner $y = 180$	7.76	4.62	3.26
Leave corner $y = 180$	8.70	5.02	3.44
Reach corner $y = 600$	26.20	15.52	10.92
Leave corner $y = 600$	31.42	17.78	11.92

The differences in the wage ranges for which the kinks and jumps are relevant are shown in Table 4.4. This gives the wage levels at which individuals move to or from the earnings thresholds of the tax and transfer system, for alternative values of the preference parameter, α. The values of the elasticities over the various ranges are found to be quite similar, and of course they are all -1 at the corners with $y = 180$ and $y = 600$, but the table shows that the main differences relate to the relevant wage ranges. For example, with a lower leisure preference (higher α) individuals start work at lower wage rates. The impact of α, therefore, is that different values tend to cause individuals' elasticity schedules (such as that shown in Figure 4.2) to shift left or right rather than alter shape.

Returning to Table 4.3, two features stand out. Firstly, allowing for endogenous labour supply has a noticeable effect on the magnitudes of both tax revenue elasticity measures: $\eta_{T_Y,W}$ rises from 1.468 to 2.095 as α is reduced from 0.9 to 0.1, with a slightly smaller increase in $\eta_{T_Y,Y}$. Secondly, the extent to which $\eta_{T_Y,W}$ exceeds the more commonly calculated $\eta_{T_Y,Y}$ also depends on the nature of leisure preferences. With a strong preference for consumption (high α) the increase in tax revenues is only about 6 per cent higher using $\eta_{T_Y,W}$ compared with the use of $\eta_{T_Y,Y}$, whereas with a stronger leisure preference (low α), this figure is around 30 per cent. This suggests that the accurate measurement of $\eta_{T_Y,W}$ in practice is likely to require an allowance for population heterogeneity.

4.4   Conclusions

This chapter has suggested that the usual practice of estimating the revenue responsiveness of income tax using the elasticity of tax revenue with respect to income (earnings) may be misleading as a guide to how tax revenue responds to changes in wage rates. Analytical expressions for these elasticities have typically treated earnings as exogenous, so that they do not accommodate the endogenous response of labour supply to the income tax system. This chapter has shown how revenue elasticity expressions can be adapted to allow for wage growth and endogenous labour supply. The primary objective was to identify how far, and in what circumstances, labour supply effects are quantitatively important for revenue responsiveness estimates, both for individual taxpayers and in aggregate.

Analytical elasticity expressions in section 4.1 showed the importance of the income tax structure, defined in terms of tax rates and thresholds, the elasticity of income tax allowances with respect to wages, and the labour supply elasticity. The last of these is, in turn, a function of the tax structure and leisure preferences, in addition to the wage structure. In order to quantify these various determinants, a numerical exercise was used based on a stylised version of the UK income tax and transfer system. For individuals, this showed that even a relatively simple tax–benefit structure can produce labour supply responses which considerably alter tax revenue elasticity calculations. Especially for individuals on low wages where income taxes and transfers interact, and for those close to income tax thresholds, tax–income elasticities can severely misrepresent tax–wage responses. At most wage levels, however, and with modest leisure preferences ($\alpha = 0.5$), tax–wage elasticities were between 3 per cent and 10 per cent higher than tax–income elasticities, when allowing for endogenous labour supply.

Aggregate tax revenue elasticities were also computed for a simulated sample of individuals, using a lognormal distribution of wage rates. The results suggested that, in aggregate, tax–income elasticities may provide a reasonable approximation of tax–wage responses but only in the presence of a strong preference for consumption over leisure. With α around 0.5 or lower, aggregate income tax revenue growth associated with a given increase in wage rates can be as much as 30 per cent greater than the response of tax revenues to earned incomes. Recent estimates of the labour supply responses of men on average in the UK are generally small and positive, which might suggest that an exogeneity assumption is a reasonable approximation when estimating tax elasticities. However, it is also known that labour supply responses for particular groups of individuals (such as women, pension recipients, and low-wage men) can differ widely. Furthermore, aggregate tax revenue elasticities depend on the proportions of the population who are near the labour supply jump points in the budget set (arising from entry into the labour market and non–convexities), where the labour supply elasticity is high, and near the kinks arising from increasing marginal tax rates, where the elasticity is -1. This suggests that empirical estimation of tax revenue elasticities may have to be aware of the differential impact of wage growth for different types of individual.

Appendix 4.1: Taxation and Labour Supply

This appendix provides a brief diagrammatic treatment of labour supply with piecewise–linear budget constraints made up of several linear segments, each associated with a given marginal tax rate and earnings threshold. The analysis assumes that the individual has a fixed gross wage in a single job. Each individual is assumed to maximise utility, regarded as a function of net income and leisure, subject to a budget constraint.

A simple nonlinear constraint is shown in Figure 4.8 as ABC, which has a kink at B, reflecting the presence of an earnings threshold where the marginal effective tax rate increases. The budget set is convex: a straight line joining any two points is associated with a feasible position, that is a net income less than or equal to the net income along the budget line. The earnings threshold is not evident from the budget constraint, since the hours level at which it occurs depends on the wage rate. For a higher wage rate, the budget constraint pivots to $AB'C'$, and the kink point B' is to the left of B. This is because a lower hours level is required, at the higher wage, to reach the earnings threshold where the marginal rate increases; gross and thus net income remain constant at the kink.

A corner solution is shown in Figure 4.9, where the highest indifference curve just touches the budget constraint at point B. However, the optimal position for the individual can nevertheless be represented as if it were a tangency solution. The artificial budget line can be drawn which is tangential to the indifference curve at the kink, B. This generates the important concepts of the virtual wage and virtual income.

The relationship between gross earnings (the product of hours worked and the gross wage, that is, wh) and the wage rate is shown in Figure 4.10. At very low wages, utility maximisation gives rise to the corner solution at A. When the wage rate exceeds some level (as the section AB of the constraint pivots about A), the individual moves to a tangency position.

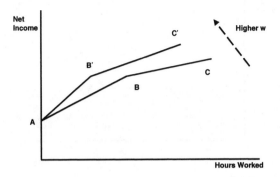

Figure 4.8: A Convex Budget Set

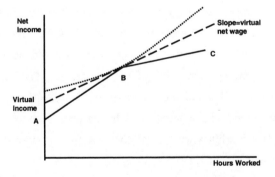

Figure 4.9: A Corner Solution

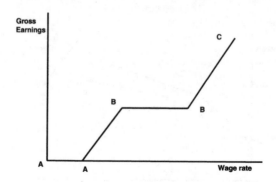

Figure 4.10: Gross Earnings and the Wage Rate

Increases in the wage induce higher labour supply until the gross earnings threshold is reached at which the marginal effective tax rate increases. A characteristic of this kind of kink in the budget constraint – where there is no tangency solution but a position where the highest indifference curve touches the relevant corner – is that the individual 'sticks' at the corner for a range of wage rates. In this case the gross earnings remain constant as the wage rate rises over a range, although of course the associated hours level falls. Eventually, for a sufficiently high wage rate, the individual moves to a tangency along the range BC of the constraint. The lengths of the flat sections AA and BB, and the nature of the rising sections AB and BC, depend on the individual's preferences. A higher preference for consumption over leisure (flatter indifference curves) gives rise to shorter sections AA and BB in Figure 4.10.

Individuals may face the same tax rates and thresholds, but the variation in non–wage incomes, wage rates and preferences means that each budget constraint and gross earnings/wage schedule is unique. However, the existence of the kink may suggest some bunching of individuals around the threshold in the distribution of gross earnings. This kind of phenomenon is nevertheless only observed in particular cases – a tax threshold need not

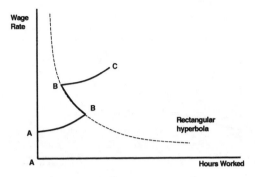

Figure 4.11: Labour Supply Curve With a Corner Solution

produce a 'spike' in the earnings distribution, and modes may in practice correspond to tangency solutions. Hence, the distribution of earnings need not necessarily provide any information about the extent of the labour supply effects of taxation.

The range BB in Figure 4.10 is associated with a fixed level of earnings, so that wh is constant. This implies that, in a graph of hours worked plotted against the wage rate, the hours of work would follow a rectangular hyperbola over the relevant range. The labour supply function is shown in Figure 4.11. This property, that the labour supply curve turns sharply backwards, following a rectangular hyperbola, as the wage rate increases over a range, is entirely general and applies to any kink in the budget constraint associated with an increase in the marginal effective tax rate at a threshold level of earnings. Thus, it makes little sense to attempt to describe the labour supply function (hours supplied as a function of the gross wage) in terms of a single elasticity. Even if the ranges AB and BC have a constant elasticity, large variations occur at the kink points, and of course the elasticity changes sign twice.

An example of a budget constraint with a means–tested benefit is given in Figure 4.12, as ABC. The benefit is gradually withdrawn at a relatively

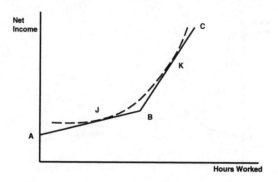

Figure 4.12: Means–testing: A Non–convex Budget Set

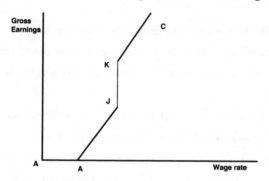

Figure 4.13: Gross Earnings and the Wage Rate

high rate until it is exhausted at B, when the individual only pays income tax: the budget set is said to be non–convex. This raises the possibility of an indifference curve being simultaneously tangential to the two sections of the constraint, for a particular wage rate; this is shown in Figure 4.12 by the two tangencies at J and K. A small increase in the wage rate would therefore produce a discrete jump in hours worked from J to K.

A discrete jump of this kind is reflected in the relationship between gross earnings and the wage rate, shown in Figure 4.13. When the wage rate is increased, earnings become positive after a particular wage has been passed

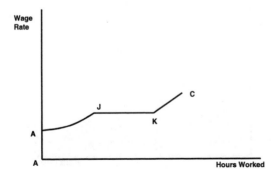

Figure 4.14: Labour Supply Curve with a Means–tested Benefit

and the individual increases labour supply along the range AB. But at a particular wage, the 'switching' wage, the individual jumps to point K along the range BC in Figure 4.13. Further increases in the wage produce a gradual increase in labour supply along KC. The associated labour supply curve is shown in Figure 4.14, where the vertical jump in Figure 4.13 translates into a horizontal range of the supply curve. There is a range where the individual is working and receiving benefits along part of AJ; but this is just a proportion of the hours range over which the individual is actually eligible for benefits.

These properties of the relationship between the shape of the budget constraint and the labour supply curve are completely general: a kink in the budget constraint associated with a rise in the marginal tax rate is associated with a 'backwards bending' range along a rectangular hyperbola (where gross earnings are constant), and a kink associated with a fall in the effective marginal tax rate produces a horizontal range in the supply curve. In the first case the kink produces a degree of rigidity (no movement from the 'travelling' kink as the wage changes), while in the second case the kink produces a discrete jump in labour supply.

The existence of means–testing may actually rule out a complete section of the budget line from the point of view of labour supply. Such a possibility

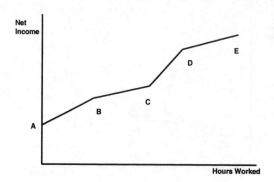

Figure 4.15: A Multi-rate System

arises where, instead of two tangency positions, the highest indifference curve gives rise simultaneously to a corner solution at A and a tangency at K. Hence the whole range of AB is ruled out, as well as the range BK of BC in Figure 4.12. The individual would not be observed both working and receiving the means–tested benefit, that is, would not be among the 'working poor'.

Figure 4.15 contains a budget constraint having four marginal tax rates. Means–testing of benefits involves an increase in the marginal rate after point B, and a subsequent reduction in the marginal rate once benefits have been exhausted at point C. The range DE reflects an increase in the marginal income tax rate beyond D. This degree of nonlinearity of the budget constraint generates the possibility of multiple local optima on different ranges of the constraint. Figure 4.16 shows a situation where indifference curve U_1 is tangential to the budget constraint along CD, while curve U_2 gives a corner solution at point B where higher taper or benefit withdrawal rates start to apply. This does not introduce any new principles, but raises complications when modelling labour supply, as care must be taken to select the global optimum.

The labour supply curve resulting from this four–rate tax structure is shown in Figure 4.17. This reflects the general properties obtained above.

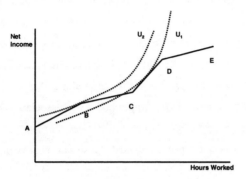

Figure 4.16: Multiple Local Optima

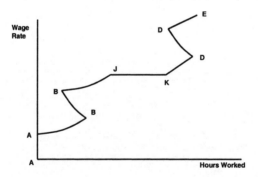

Figure 4.17: Labour Supply Curve with a Multi-rate Tax System

Hence the two corners B and D of the constraint (and the earnings thresholds associated with them) in Figure 4.15 generate the two ranges BB and DD of Figure 4.17 which involve reductions in labour supply along rectangular hyperbolae. The flat section of the supply curve JK is associated with the jump from a tangency along BC to a tangency along DC of the budget constraint. The rising sections of the supply curve are associated with tangency solutions.

The supply curve need not necessarily take the precise form shown in Figure 4.17. Consider again the budget constraint shown in Figure 4.14. The supply curve may involve, for a small increase in the wage rate, a jump directly from a corner solution at point B on the budget constraint to a tangency along the length CD of the constraint. This is more likely to occur, the higher is the benefit withdrawal rate (the flatter the segment AB). Furthermore, it is quite possible that a jump could occur from the kink in the budget constraint at B directly to the kink at D, thereby leaving out the whole of the range of the constraint from B to D.

Appendix 4.2: The Tax Structure and Budget Constraints

This appendix explains how the thresholds and rates which define a tax and transfer system can be converted to a budget constraint for an individual facing a given gross wage rate. Given a gross wage rate, w, the thresholds and marginal tax rates must be transformed into a set of virtual incomes, m_k, and net wages, $w(1 - t_k)$, which describe respectively the intercept and the slope of each of the K linear segments of the budget constraint.

The virtual income at the start of the first segment of the budget constraint, m_1, must be known. If there are no other sources of income, such as transfer payments or income from non–wage sources, and it is required to model only an income tax, then m_1 is set to zero. This corresponds to net income when the individual does not work. Along the kth linear segment, net income, z, corresponding to h hours of work is:

$$z = m_k + w(1 - t_k)h \tag{4.24}$$

Let h_k^* denote the hours of work for which gross earnings are equal to the specified gross earnings thresholds. Clearly, $h_1^* = 0$, and for $k > 1$, given that two adjacent segments k and $k - 1$ must intersect at point h_k^* (assuming that there are no discontinuities), it must be true that:

$$m_k + w(1 - t_k)h_k^* = m_{k-1} + w(1 - t_{k-1})h_k^* \tag{4.25}$$

Hence, for $k = 2, ..., K$:

$$h_k^* = \frac{m_k - m_{k-1}}{w(t_k - t_{k-1})} \tag{4.26}$$

Next, consider the net incomes at the earnings thresholds. For $k = 1$, $a_1 = 0$, and $z = m_1$. At a_2 net income is $m_1 + a_2(1 - t_1)$ and for $k = 3, ..., K$:

$$z = m_1 + \sum_{j=2}^{k-1} a_j(t_j - t_{j-1}) + a_k(1 - t_{k-1}) \tag{4.27}$$

Equating these with the corresponding values of $m_{k-1} + w\,(1 - t_{k-1})\,h_k^*$, and substituting for h_k^* from (4.26), it can be seen that, for $k = 2, ..., K$:

$$m_k = m_{k-1} + a_k(t_k - t_{k-1}) \tag{4.28}$$

The piecewise–linear budget constraint for any value of w, corresponding to a given set of a_k and t_k (along with m_1) is thus fully defined. The net tax paid can be expressed in terms of the difference between gross earnings and net income at the corresponding level of hours worked, and is $y - \{m_k + w(1 - t_k)h\}$.

Part III

Applications

Chapter 5

Income and Consumption Taxes in the UK

This chapter provides estimates of the revenue elasticity of income and consumption taxes (VAT and the main excises) with respect to changes in income in the UK since the end of the 1980s. Using the analysis developed in Part II, it concentrates on income and consumption taxes, which together account for around 55 per cent of total tax revenues in the UK. The other main tax revenue contributors, not analysed here, are National Insurance Contributions (17 per cent) and corporation tax (10 per cent). Modelling the revenue elasticities of National Insurance Contributions is complicated by the need to specify differences of contracting–in and contracting–out rates across the income distribution and the variety of employer contribution rates. In the case of corporation tax, elasticity estimates would require modelling of the company tax base – profits, interest payments and so on. The analysis below therefore abstracts from these taxes.

An important feature of income tax revenue elasticity estimates for the UK is the imporance of allowing for changes in income-related deductions. Furthermore, changes in income tax revenue elasticities over the period are decomposed into effects associated with changes in the tax structure, real income growth and inflation. For consumption tax revenue elasticities, chapter 3 demonstrated that these are affected by consumption patterns and savings rates. This chapter shows that allowing for changes in these consumption patterns over time, and differential savings rates across individuals, is important for revenue elasticity estimates in the UK context. Values of elasticities at both the individual and aggregate levels are reported below.

Estimates of revenue elasticities are an important input into the debate on changes in the burden of taxation in the UK. Because these estimates are based on a constant tax structure, they enable observed changes in average tax levels to be decomposed into those arising directly from budgetary changes and those which result from the tax system's built-in flexibility, in the absence of discretionary changes. Clarke *et al.* (2002), for example, draw attention to the fact that real alcohol and tobacco duties have risen substantially since 1996/97, yet the share of these taxes in GDP has remained constant or declined. Revenue elasticity estimates help to identify how far such revenue changes represent built-in effects related to the structure of these and other taxes.

Tax revenue elasticities also provide vital inputs into a number of tax forecasting models in the UK where, in association with assumptions regarding tax base changes, they generate revenue growth predictions for given tax policies. Tax forecasting models for income and corporation taxes produced by the Institute for Fiscal Studies (IFS), for example, estimate or use revenue elasticities; see Giles and Hall (1998) and Sentance *et al.* (1998). Despite their usefulness, there are surprisingly few published tax revenue elasticity estimates for the UK. Values for the 1980–1984 period were provided by Johnson and Lambert (1989) but these relate to income taxes only. This neglect may reflect the perception that, in the presence of lower rates of inflation in recent years, fiscal drag is no longer significant; see Heinemann (2001). However, from the mid-1980s, major changes have taken place to the income tax structure involving a simplification of tax rates and allowances, the reduction and elimination of mortgage tax relief and, more recently, the extension of allowances and deductions for pension contributions, savings and families.

There have also been changes in consumption taxes such as VAT and excise taxes particularly on tobacco and petrol, and the taxation of domestic fuel. However, the share of consumption taxes has remained approximately 30 per cent of general government revenue. These policy changes are likely to have affected both income and consumption tax revenue elasticities and are examined in detail in this chapter.

5.1   Revenue and Income Changes

Evidence on aggregate income and consumption tax levels is given in Table 5.1. Annual data in this chapter refer to fiscal years: for example, 1998 is the year from 6 April 1998 to 5 April 1999. Two different data sources are used. Data on total income and income tax revenue in columns two and three are taken from *Inland Revenue Statistics* and the final two columns are from *Economic Trends*. (VAT, excise and other indirect taxes are referred to here as consumption taxes, though the Office of National Statistics uses the term production taxes). The lower section of the table reports buoyancy estimates; that is, the ratio of the change in revenue to the change in aggregate income, over various periods. These values indicate both the relatively low buoyancy for income taxes throughout and the noticeably higher consumption tax buoyancy over the post-1989 period.

Rates of increase of all taxes were particularly low during the cyclical upturn in 1984–89, when income growth was temporarily high. Measured over several years, income tax revenues have generally risen only around 15–20 per cent faster than incomes. Consumption tax revenues, by contrast, have increased fairly rapidly over the last decade, increasing around 35 per cent faster than incomes. Much of this reflects the large revenue increases associated with the increased VAT rates in 1991 and 1994. However, these changes combine both discretionary and automatic effects. The primary focus of the following sections is to identify how far these observed changes

Table 5.1: Tax Revenue and Income Growth

Year	Total income	Tax revenue (£ millions)		
		Income tax	Income and wealth tax	Consumption tax
1979	102000	18500	26025	23561
1984	157000	30900	48166	44063
1989	333000	53400	73483	64537
1999	531550	92500	129145	122832
2000	556000	97000	140088	129263
Period		Buoyancy:		
1979-1984		1.189	1.427	1.452
1984-1989		0.728	0.562	0.508
1989-1999		1.175	1.206	1.376
1989-2000		1.164	1.259	1.355

reflect built-in flexibility properties of the various income and indirect taxes.

As shown in Part II, estimates of aggregate revenue elasticities can be obtained using convenient analytical expressions, which have the advantage that they can be evaluated readily from official published sources. Section 5.2 shows how this analysis can be applied to UK income tax revenue elasticities. Section 5.3 reports values for consumption taxes. Results at the individual level are then presented in section 5.4, and section 5.5 draws some conclusions.

5.2 Income Tax Revenue Elasticities

This section presents estimates of income tax revenue elasticities using the analytical expressions described in chapter 2. Since the elasticity of effective allowances is an important component of the revenue elasticity, estimates for both these elasticities are reported below. A decomposition analysis is reported in subsection 5.2.5, which highlights the importance of discretionary fiscal changes for changes in the income tax revenue elasticity.

5.2.1 Elasticity Formulae

Chapter 2 introduced the multi-step income tax function in which an individual with gross income of y_i faces an income tax function, such that if $0 < y_i \leq a_1$, the tax paid is $T_{y_i} = 0$; if $a_1 < y_i \leq a_2$, $T_{y_i} = t_1 (y_i - a_1)$; if $a_2 < y_i \leq a_3$, $T_{y_i} = t_1 (a_2 - a_1) + t_2 (y_i - a_2)$, and so on. Hence if y_i falls into the kth tax bracket, so that $a_k < y_i \leq a_{k+1}$, and $a_0 = t_0 = 0$, it was shown that income tax can be expressed, for $k \geq 1$, as:

$$
\begin{aligned}
T_{y_i} &= t_k (y_i - a_k) + \sum_{j=0}^{k-1} t_j (a_{j+1} - a_j) \\
&= t_k (y_i - a'_k)
\end{aligned}
\tag{5.1}
$$

where $a'_k = \sum_{j=1}^{k} a_j (t_j - t_{j-1}) / t_k$. The function in (5.1) is equivalent to a single-step tax structure having a marginal rate, t_k, imposed on the individual's income in excess of an effective threshold of a'_k.

A feature of income taxation in the UK during the period considered here is that, in addition to the tax thresholds determined by personal characteristics, a_j in (5.1) is also affected by numerous allowances and deductions which reduce taxable income; such as reliefs for mortgages, pension contributions and some savings schemes. In view of the fact that they are endogenous and vary systematically with individuals' incomes, it is important to remember that a'_k is a function of y_i, as well as the set of marginal income tax rates.

In chapter 2 it was shown that the individual revenue elasticity of income tax, T_{y_i} with respect to y_i, η_{T_y, y_i}, can be expressed as:

$$
\eta_{T_y, y_i} = 1 + \left(\frac{a'_k}{y_i - a'_k} \right) \left(1 - \eta_{a'_k, y_i} \right)
\tag{5.2}
$$

This shows that the elasticity must exceed unity if the elasticity of effective allowances is less than 1. Evaluation of the aggregate elasticity across all individuals requires knowledge of the extent to which individuals' incomes change when aggregate income changes. For the case of equiproportionate income growth, the aggregate elasticity is a simple tax-share weighted average of individual elasticities. This assumption is not likely to hold in general, however. For example, Clark *et al.* (2002) give summary information about differences in the average growth of incomes within different deciles of the income distribution. Though it is not explored in this chapter, it was shown in chapter 2 that the process of regression towards or away from mean incomes over time can be incorporated readily into revenue elasticity estimates. The method is applied to New Zealand in chapter 7, where it is shown that systematic equalising changes in incomes have the effect of reducing aggregate revenue elasticities, though these appear in general not to be sensitive to the kinds of annual changes in inequality observed in practice.

5.2.2 Income Distributions and Tax Structures

The UK income tax structure in recent years has taken a two–step or three–step form. Computation of the aggregate revenue elasticity requires information about tax rates and allowances and the distribution of incomes in each year. This section uses annual data on the distribution of taxpayers' incomes from *Inland Revenue Statistics* (IRS) for 1989–2000. These data are not available at the individual level, but cover all taxpayers sorted into 15 income groups for most years. In 1992, 1997 and 1998 there were 14 groups, and in 1989 there were 16 income groups. The year 1998 is the last for which these income distribution data were available. Since the lower income limit in IRS income distribution data for each year is that year's single person's allowance, this is also used to measure the a_js in equation (5.1). Using the married person's allowance makes little difference to the revenue elasticity estimates reported below. Furthermore, the declining (tax credit) value and recent withdrawal of the married allowance for almost all married taxpayers means that revenue elasticity estimates for recent years would be unaffected. Age-related allowances have been ignored in the calculations.

The IRS data are used to obtain the mean and variance of the logarithms of the income distribution for each year, and these values are used to parameterise a simulated lognormal income distribution. Income tax rates and thresholds and the means and variances of log-incomes for each year are given in Table 5.2. In the absence of suitable distributional data, the values of the variance of log–income for 1999–2000 are taken as being the same as in 1998. Each revenue elasticity is then obtained using a simulated population of 20,000 individuals, drawn at random from the appropriate lognormal distribution. This gives exactly the same results as obtained using analytical results based on the properties of the lognormal, using the expressions given in chapter 2. However, the simulated values are necessary here for the subsequent computation of consumption tax revenue elasticities.

5.2.3   Effective Allowance Elasticities

Equation (5.2) shows that when there are income-related deductions, their income elasticity, $\eta_{a'_k, y_i}$, can have an important effect on the elasticity of tax revenues. Annual estimates of $\eta_{a'_k, y_i}$ were obtained from IRS data on allowances and deductions, by income group, using regressions of the form:

$$\log a'_{kj} = \alpha + \beta \log y_j \tag{5.3}$$

where there are $j = 1, ..., n$ income groups. Estimates of the coefficient β provide estimates of the required (constant) elasticity $\eta_{a'_k, y_i}$. Since a'_{kj} takes discrete jumps at income levels where higher marginal income tax rates apply, up to two dummy variables were added to these regressions to allow for these discrete changes. The use of a double–log specification is similar to that followed by Johnson and Lambert (1989) who used Family Expenditure Survey (FES) data for a single year. In view of the considerable changes to the form of income–related deductions from the early 1990s, new annual estimates of $\eta_{a'_k, y_i}$ are required. Johnson and Lambert's (1989) estimate of 0.58 for the income elasticity of deductions is not directly comparable with that obtained here since they use the 'subpopulation of deduction takers', rather than all taxpayers or income recipients, as the basis for their regression estimates. Their use of FES data is also likely to produce rather different outcomes to those obtained here from IRS data.

Details of regressions based on equation (5.3), to generate values of the elasticity of effective allowances, are reported in Table 5.3; the elasticities are illustrated in Figure 5.1. Regressions for each year are based on cross–sections of up to 16 income groups. Two values are reported for 1997: omitting the top income group from the 1997 cross–section data was found to reduce the income parameter substantially, from 0.347 to 0.216. A compromise estimate of 0.25 was used in revenue elasticity calculations.

The elasticity of allowances with respect to income declined from 0.45 in 1989 to around 0.2 in 1994, thereafter stabilising and rising slightly to around 0.26 in 1998. Data on the composition of deductions, summarised in Table 5.4, reveals that the declining value of $\eta_{a'_k, y_i}$ to 1994 largely reflects the falling real value of mortgage interest tax relief. Further falls thereafter are masked by the introduction of mortgage interest relief at source (MIRAS) in 1993 and 1994 such that mortgage interest tax relief dropped out of the deductions data from 1994. However, even if MIRAS were included in deductions data after 1994, it would represent a declining share, until mortgage interest became ineligible for tax relief after 1999. Occupational and personal pension deductions, which disproportionately benefit those on higher incomes, dominate the total deductions data from 1994.

5.2.4   Income Tax Revenue Elasticities

The aggregate income tax revenue elasticities for each year were obtained by first computing individual values from equation (5.2). The individual values of y_i were obtained using a simulated population of 20,000 individuals drawn at random from a lognormal income distribution, with mean and variance of

Table 5.2: Income Tax Structures and Income Distribution Parameters

	Marginal Rates			Income Thresholds				
year	t_1	t_2	t_3	a_1	a_2	a_3	μ	σ^2
1989	0.25	0.4	–	2785	23485	–	9.323	0.472
1990	0.25	0.4	–	3005	23705	–	9.246	0.438
1991	0.25	0.4	–	3295	26995	–	9.308	0.434
1992	0.2	0.25	0.4	3445	5445	27145	9.336	0.431
1993	0.2	0.25	0.4	3445	5945	27145	9.356	0.433
1994	0.2	0.25	0.4	3445	6445	27145	9.375	0.438
1995	0.2	0.25	0.4	3525	6725	27825	9.403	0.446
1996	0.2	0.24	0.4	3765	7665	29265	9.459	0.448
1997	0.2	0.23	0.4	4045	8145	30145	9.509	0.445
1998	0.2	0.23	0.4	4195	8495	31295	9.555	0.456
1999	0.1	0.23	0.4	4335	5835	32335	9.583	0.456
2000	0.1	0.22	0.4	4385	5905	32785	9.611	0.456

Table 5.3: Effective Allowance Regressions

Year	β	Std. error	R^2	n
1989	0.450	0.045	0.98	16
1990	0.379	0.025	0.99	15
1991	0.370	0.017	0.99	15
1992	0.331	0.015	0.99	14
1993	0.275	0.026	0.99	15
1994	0.212	0.016	0.99	15
1995	0.214	0.021	0.99	15
1996	0.265	0.021	0.99	15
1997	0.347	0.039	0.99	14
1997	0.216	0.032	0.99	13
1998	0.264	0.026	0.99	14

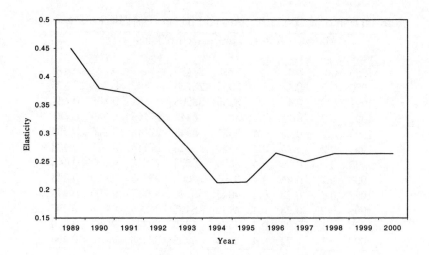

Figure 5.1: Elasticity of Allowances

Table 5.4: Income Tax Deductions

Year	Total Deductions £bn.	Mortgage Interest %	Occupational Pensions %	Personal Pensions %	Other Deductions %
1990	39.6	66	19	8	6
1992	34.8	56	24	13	7
1994	16.3	–	54	31	15
1996	18.6	–	52	34	14
1998	21.7	–	51	34	15
2000	23.6	–	58	33	9

Table 5.5: Income Tax Revenue Elasticities

year	$\eta_{a'_k,y_i}$	$\eta_{T_Y,Y}$ $(\eta_{a'_k,y_i} = 0)$	$\eta_{T_Y,Y}$ $(\eta_{a'_k,y_i} > 0)$
1989	0.450	1.380	1.209
1990	0.379	1.418	1.260
1991	0.370	1.418	1.263
1992	0.331	1.468	1.313
1993	0.275	1.471	1.341
1994	0.212	1.473	1.373
1995	0.214	1.472	1.371
1996	0.265	1.487	1.358
1997	0.250	1.501	1.376
1998	0.264	1.497	1.366
1999	0.264	1.529	1.389
2000	0.264	1.538	1.396

logarithms for each year given by the values reported in Table 5.2. Second, the aggregate elasticities were constructed from the resulting individual elasticity values based on the tax–share weighted average described in chapter 2 for the equiproportionate income growth case (that is, where $\eta_{y_i,Y} = 1$ for all i).

Table 5.5 shows the resulting income tax revenue elasticities over the 1989–2000 period. For each year, two values of $\eta_{T_Y,Y}$ are reported. Column 4 uses the deductions elasticities reported in column 2, and shows that the revenue elasticity increased from 1.2 in 1989 to about 1.4 by 2000. Column 3 demonstrates the importance of allowing for the deductions elasticity effect. Ignoring this, by setting $\eta_{a'_k,y_i} = 0$ for all individuals, increases the revenue elasticity substantially to 1.38 in 1989, rising to 1.54 in 2000. Figure 5.2 shows the two sets of income tax revenue elasticities over the 1989–2000 period; that is, using the assumption that $\eta_{a'_k,y} = 0$ for all individuals, as well as using the estimates of $\eta_{a'_k,y}$ presented above.

These values may be compared with results from earlier studies. Using rough estimates of aggregate effective average and marginal tax rates of ap-

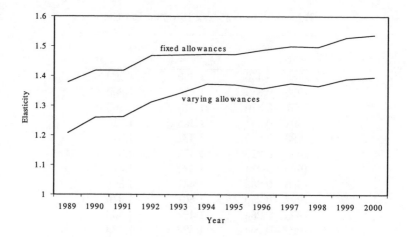

Figure 5.2: Income Tax Revenue Elasticities

proximately 17 and 27 per cent respectively, Robinson (1987) suggested that
the aggregate income tax revenue elasticity was around 1.6 during the early
1980s. Johnson and Lambert (1989) confirmed estimates in the region of 1.5
to 1.64 for 1980–84. With the decline in the marginal tax rate faced by most
taxpayers since that period, and the rise in real incomes relative to tax thresholds, it might be expected that the income tax revenue elasticity would fall.
However, both marginal *and* average rates have fallen over this period, with
the *relative* changes in these determining changes in the revenue elasticity.
Nevertheless, the evidence presented here suggests that income tax revenue
elasticities since 1989 were well below the earlier estimates, but appear to
have been rising during the 1990s.

5.2.5 Decomposing the Revenue Elasticity

Though revenue elasticities capture the effects of automatic revenue changes,
as equation (5.2) makes clear these elasticities are also affected by discre-

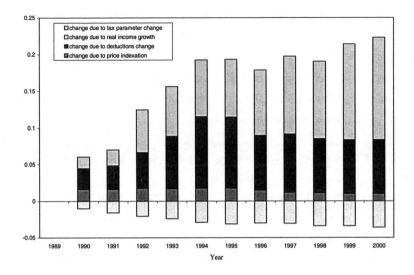

Figure 5.3: Decomposition of Changes in Income Tax Revenue Elasticities

tionary changes in the tax structure. Indeed, changes in the revenue elasticity can be decomposed into changes due to the growth of nominal incomes (including both real and inflationary components), alterations to tax rates and thresholds, and changes in the deduction–income relationship, caused by fiscal decisions and endogenous responses by taxpayers.

These decompositions are illustrated in Figure 5.3. This shows that the observed change in the revenue elasticity is substantially due to fiscal decisions which changed both the deductions–income elasticity and income tax rates and allowances. Other things equal, real income growth would have reduced the revenue elasticity slightly (by around 0.04 by 2000), with inflation having an even smaller positive effect. This evidence can be interpreted as consistent with that of Heinemann (2001) who found, using a regression approach, that there was no significant fiscal drag, either nominal or real, in the UK during 1972–96. However, Heinemann's evidence is based on the assumption of constant elasticities of revenue with respect to real income and prices. Figure 5.3 also shows that the Labour government's income tax reforms in 1999 and 2000 (over–indexing thresholds and reducing the standard and lower tax rates), had the effect of increasing the income tax system's revenue responsiveness, even though the immediate impact would be some reduction in income tax revenues.

5.3 Consumption Tax Revenue Elasticities

Chapter 3 gave a detailed derivation of the consumption tax revenue elasticity, demonstrating that this depends on the extent to which an individual's net income changes as gross income changes and, in turn, on the way in which consumption expenditure responds to changes in net income. In addition, consumption tax revenue elasticities depend on the precise structure of consumption taxes. This section provides estimates for UK consumption-tax revenue elasticities during 1989–2000. First, subsection 5.3.1 summarises the key conceptual expressions; subsection 5.3.2 discusses the specification of the consumption function to be applied in this case; and subsection 5.3.3 outlines the data to be used. Elasticity estimates are then discussed in subsection 5.3.4.

5.3.1 Elasticity Formulae

Define z_i as net income, so that:

$$\begin{aligned} z_i &= y_i - T\left(y_i, a'_k\right) \\ &= a'_k t_k + y_i \left(1 - t_k\right) \end{aligned} \tag{5.4}$$

Letting a proportion, γ_i, of z_i be consumed, total consumption expenditure by the individual, m_i, is:

$$m_i = \gamma_i z_i \tag{5.5}$$

In general, the term γ_i can vary with z_i and hence with y_i, as discussed in chapter 3.

Suppose that the tax–exclusive indirect tax rate imposed on the ℓth good (for $\ell = 1, ..., n$) is v_ℓ, giving rise to the equivalent tax–inclusive rate of $v'_\ell = v_\ell / (1 + v_\ell)$. Define $w_{i\ell}$ as the individual's budget share of the ℓth good. The consumption tax paid on all goods, T_{iv}, is given by:

$$T_{v_i} = m_i \sum_{\ell=1}^{n} v'_\ell w_{i\ell} \tag{5.6}$$

Given these expressions for T_{v_i}, m_i, and z_i, chapter 3 demonstrated that the elasticity of T_v, with respect to gross income, y_i, η_{T_v, y_i}, can be expressed as:

$$\eta_{T_v, y_i} = \eta_{m_i, y_i} \left\{ \sum_{\ell=1}^{n} \left(\frac{T_{i\ell}}{T_{v_i}} \right) e_{i\ell} \right\} \tag{5.7}$$

where the term in curly brackets is the weighted sum of the expenditure elasticities, $e_{i\ell}$, with weights given by the share of each tax in total consumption tax revenue. Further, from (5.5), it is possible to express η_{m_i, y_i} as:

$$\eta_{m_i, y_i} = \eta_{\gamma_i, y_i} + \eta_{z_i, y_i} \tag{5.8}$$

so that (5.7) can be written as

$$\eta_{T_v, y_i} = \left(\eta_{\gamma_i, y_i} + \eta_{z, y_i} \right) \left\{ \sum_{\ell=1}^{n} \left(\frac{T_{i\ell}}{T_{v_i}} \right) e_{i\ell} \right\} \tag{5.9}$$

Chapter 3 then showed that the elasticity of net income with respect to gross income, η_{z_i, y_i}, is simply the familiar measure of residual progression of the income tax, such that (5.9) becomes:

$$\eta_{T_v, y_i} = \left(\eta_{\gamma_i, y_i} + \frac{1 - mtr_{y_i}}{1 - atr_{y_i}} \right) \left\{ \sum_{\ell=1}^{n} \left(\frac{T_{i\ell}}{T_{v_i}} \right) e_{i\ell} \right\} \tag{5.10}$$

Before (5.10) can be applied to data, it is necessary to specify the form of the consumption function in order to determine values of the consumption proportion elasticity, η_{γ_i, y_i}. This is examined in the next subsection.

5.3.2 The Consumption Function

In the above formulation, the individual's expenditure proportion, γ_i, may vary with income. There are a number of possible forms for this relationship but suppose that:

$$m_i = a\left(z_i + b\right) \tag{5.11}$$

This allows for the possibility that there is some non–proportionality in the relationship between expenditure and net income. This is often observed in practice, for example, because of transfers received by those on low incomes and because of higher savings rates by those on higher incomes. Using (5.5) and (5.11) gives:

$$\gamma_i = \frac{m_i}{z_i} = a\left(1 + \frac{b}{y_i - T_{y_i}}\right) \tag{5.12}$$

Differentiating (5.12), and using (5.8) and (5.9) it can be shown that:

$$
\begin{aligned}
\eta_{m_i,y_i} &= \eta_{z,y_i}\left(1 - \frac{b}{y_i - T_{y_i} + b}\right) \\
&= \eta_{z,y_i}\left(1 - \frac{ab}{m_i}\right) \tag{5.13}
\end{aligned}
$$

which may be used to substitute for η_{m_i,y_i} in (5.7) to give the individual consumption tax revenue elasticity as:

$$\eta_{T_v,y_i} = \left(1 - \frac{ab}{m_i}\right)\left(\frac{1 - mtr_{y_i}}{1 - atr_{y_i}}\right)\left\{\sum_{\ell=1}^{n}\left(\frac{T_{i\ell}}{T_{v_i}}\right)e_{i\ell}\right\} \tag{5.14}$$

This shows that the consumption tax revenue elasticity has three components. These are: the parameters (a, b) of the consumption relationship (that is, the extent of any non–proportionality between disposable income and consumption), the residual progression of the income tax structure measured by $(1 - mtr_{y_i})/(1 - atr_{y_i})$, and the tax–share weighted average elasticity of demand for each taxed good, with respect to total expenditure. Alternative specifications of the relationship between income and expenditure can be used, which affects the form of the first term in (5.14). However, the linear form appears to work well in the UK case. The first two terms of equation (5.14) are less than or equal to unity, but the third component may exceed unity for some income levels and tax structures. However, η_{T_v,y_i} tends towards unity as income increases. This is because all expenditure elasticities converge towards unity, along with the first two terms in (5.14).

To see the intuition behind these elasticity expressions it is easiest to work with the simplified case where allowances are fixed, so that $\eta_{a'_k,y_i} = 0$ for all individuals, and there is no saving; that is, $b = 0$; $a = 1$. In this special case, the individual consumption tax elasticity becomes:

$$\eta_{T_v,y_i} = \frac{y_i(1-t_k)}{m_i} \left\{ \sum_{\ell=1}^{n} \left(\frac{T_{i\ell}}{T_{v_i}}\right) e_{i\ell} \right\} \tag{5.15}$$

Equation (5.15) shows that an increase in income relative to expenditure, y_i/m_i, or a reduction in the marginal income tax rate, t_k, both serve to increase the consumption tax revenue elasticity. On the expenditure side, the revenue elasticity is higher the greater are the expenditure elasticities, $e_{i\ell}$, and tax revenue shares, $T_{i\ell}/T_{v_i}$, of taxed goods.

Finally, to estimate consumption tax elasticities for all individuals combined, define aggregate consumption tax revenue as T_V. Chapter 3 showed that the aggregate consumption tax elasticity is:

$$\eta_{T_V,Y} = \sum_{i=1}^{N} \left(\frac{T_{v_i}}{T_V}\right) \eta_{T_v,y_i} \eta_{y_i,Y} \tag{5.16}$$

where y_i is income received by individual i. Hence, as with income taxation, the aggregate consumption tax elasticity can be calculated as the consumption tax-share weighted average of the individual elasticities, provided equiproportionate income growth, $\eta_{y_i,Y} = 1$, can be assumed. Furthermore, if $T = T_Y + T_V$, the elasticity of total revenue with respect to aggregate income is:

$$\eta_{T,Y} = \left(\frac{T_Y}{T}\right) \eta_{T_Y,Y} + \left(\frac{T_V}{T}\right) \eta_{T_V,Y} \tag{5.17}$$

which is a tax–share weighted average of the income and consumption tax revenue elasticities.

5.3.3 Tax and Budget–share Data

Inspection of equation (5.14) reveals that estimation of the elasticity, η_{T_v, y_i}, requires information on the relevant budget shares and total expenditure elasticities, the relationship between m_i and z_i, and income and consumption tax parameters. For the purposes of estimating budget shares and expenditure elasticities, it is necessary to distinguish only between goods with different indirect tax rates. For example, all expenditure items subject to VAT at 17.5 per cent, and not liable to other taxes, can be treated as a single item. Since the analysis here deals only with the revenue effects of consumption taxes, the impact on final goods prices of excises levied on inputs, such as fuel duty, can legitimately be ignored. Tax incidence conclusions should not therefore be drawn from this evidence.

With the exception of savings proportions, the required information is readily available annually by income group, or can be calculated, from family expenditure surveys, Inland Revenue, UK Treasury and other official sources. Using these data, aggregate revenue elasticities for consumption taxes are obtainable from the IRS taxpayer income distribution, as the tax revenue share weighted sum of the revenue elasticities for each income group; see (5.16).

To compute the values reported below, annual FES data were used to calculate budget shares and expenditure elasticities for each of a range of total expenditure groups, distinguishing between 10 groups of consumer goods currently subject to different levels of indirect tax. The categories are: goods subject to VAT at the standard rate of 17.5 per cent; domestic fuel and power which are currently subject to VAT of 5 per cent; those for which VAT is zero–rated or exempt (non–VAT); beer; wines; spirits; other alcohol; tobacco;

motor fuel; and insurance. Though domestic fuel and power, and insurance were not subject to these tax rates throughout the period, they are examined separately for the entire 1989–2000 period so that each category is composed of the same goods throughout.

Define w_{ki} $(i = 1, ..., n)$ as the average expenditure weight, or budget share, for the ith commodity group and kth total expenditure group. Expenditure elasticities were obtained by first fitting a separate regression for each year, of the form:

$$w_{ki} = \alpha_{0,ik} + \alpha_{1,ik} \log (m_k) + \alpha_{2,ik} \left(\frac{1}{m_k} \right) \tag{5.18}$$

where m_k $(k = 1, ..., K)$ is the arithmetic mean expenditure of the kth total expenditure group.

Table 5.6 shows an example for 1999 of parameter estimates, budget shares, w, and expenditure elasticities, e, for the 10 commodity groups, using illustrative values of weekly expenditure, m, of £200 and £400. These show that the budget share regressions generally give a good fit to the data (beer is an exception). The derived expenditure elasticities are generally greater than unity at £200, except for VAT–exempts goods, tobacco and domestic fuel and power. At £400, elasticities for insurance, beer and spirits are also below unity.

Since over 80 per cent of expenditure is accounted for by non–VAT and 17.5 per cent VAT items, expenditure on those two categories is the most influential for revenue elasticity estimates. Aggregate budget shares over the period for standard rate (17.5 per cent) and non–VAT items are shown in Figure 5.4. There is a general tendency towards greater spending on VAT–liable items over time as real incomes grow. However, there is also a pronounced but temporary fall in the share of standard VAT items in 1991, and a similar rise in 1995. While the former change most likely represents a response to the increase in the standard rate of VAT in 1991, the reason for the large rise in the VAT–liable share in 1995, and its subsequent fall, is less

Table 5.6: Budget Shares and Elasticities

Categories	Parameters			R^2	$m = £200$		$m = £400$	
	α_0	α_1	α_2		w	e	w	e
non–VAT	0.569	-0.043	4.00	0.95	0.363	0.83	0.324	0.84
VAT 17.5%	-0.140	0.107	6.42	0.97	0.456	1.16	0.514	1.18
Insurance	0.062	-0.007	-2.05	0.94	0.016	1.21	0.016	0.90
Beer	0.077	-0.008	-2.27	0.17	0.025	1.14	0.026	0.92
wines	-0.034	0.007	0.86	0.97	0.006	1.41	0.009	1.53
Spirits	0.048	-0.006	-1.36	0.85	0.008	1.06	0.007	0.58
Other alcohol	0.005	-0.001	-0.37	0.73	0.001	2.12	0.002	1.30
Tobacco	0.151	-0.021	-1.94	0.99	0.028	0.59	0.018	0.10
Motor fuel	0.137	-0.013	-6.07	0.92	0.036	1.46	0.042	1.04
Dom fuel/power	0.076	-0.010	4.74	0.97	0.049	0.33	0.031	0.31

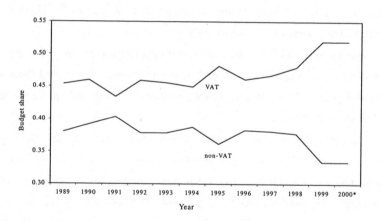

Figure 5.4: Aggregate Budget Shares for Standard and Zero–rate VAT

clear. The aggregate budget share of domestic fuel and power, not shown in Figure 5.4, fell steadily from almost 5 per cent in 1994, when 8 per cent VAT was introduced, to around 3 per cent by 2000.

Estimating the expenditure elasticities proceeds as follows. Using the basic definition $w_{ki} = p_{ki}q_{ki}/m_k$, differentiation gives:

$$\dot{w}_{ki} = \dot{m}_k (e_{ki} - 1) \tag{5.19}$$

where $\dot{w}_{ki}$ and $\dot{m}_k$ denote the proportional changes in the budget share of the ith good and total expenditure in the kth group. Hence:

$$e_{ki} = 1 + \dot{w}_{ki}/\dot{m}_k \tag{5.20}$$

Define the following discrete proportionate changes, for $k = 2, ..., K$:

$$\dot{m}'_k = (m_{k-1}/m_k) - 1 \tag{5.21}$$

$$\dot{w}'_{ki} = (w_{k-1,i}/w_{ki}) - 1 \tag{5.22}$$

so that although the dot notation has been used, the changes are obtained by comparing values in adjacent total expenditure groups. These can be used to substitute into equation (5.20) to get the set of total expenditure elasticities for $k = 2, ..., K$ and $i = 1, ..., n$, giving:

$$e'_{i(k)} = 1 + \dot{w}'_{ki}/\dot{m}'_k \tag{5.23}$$

A similar set of elasticities can be obtained, for $k = 1, ..., K - 1$, using reductions in total expenditure, such that $\dot{m}^*_k = (m_{k+1}/m_k) - 1$ and so on. Arithmetic mean values were used for $k = 2, ..., K - 1$, while elasticities corresponding respectively to downward and upward changes in m were used for $k = K$ and $k = 1$.

Details of the consumption tax structure over the period 1989 to 2000 are given in Table 5.7. Tax rates are in percentage, tax–exclusive, form; that is, they are values of $100v = 100v'/(1 - v')$. Rates for alcohol, tobacco and

Table 5.7: Consumption Tax Rates

year	VAT	insur-ance	beer	wine	spirits	other alcohol	tob-acco	petrol	dom fuel
1989	15.0	0	49.3	88.9	194.1	80.4	284.6	156.4	0
1990	15.0	0	47.1	88.9	194.1	79.1	284.6	163.2	0
1991	17.5	0	49.3	92.3	185.7	80.1	316.7	194.1	0
1992	17.5	0	49.3	92.3	194.1	81.3	316.7	203.0	0
1993	17.5	0	49.3	96.1	177.8	79.8	316.7	212.5	0
1994	17.5	5	44.9	100.0	185.7	79.3	316.7	244.8	8
1995	17.5	5	44.9	104.1	203.0	82.8	354.5	284.6	8
1996	17.5	5	44.9	104.1	185.7	80.2	354.5	316.7	8
1997	17.5	5	42.9	96.1	163.2	73.7	376.2	316.7	5
1998	17.5	5	42.9	104.1	170.3	76.7	376.2	376.2	5
1999	17.5	5	47.1	112.8	177.8	82.4	455.6	614.3	5
2000	17.5	5	47.1	117.4	170.3	82.4	614.3	733.3	5

petrol appear precise because these were calculated from tax–inclusive rates published by the IFS, see Chennels *et al.* (2000). For example, the rate of $100v = 49.25$ for beer in 1989 is equivalent to $100v' = 33$. These demonstrate both the wide variety of tax rates across expenditure items and the high rates on commodities such as tobacco and petrol. Given this wide dispersion in tax rates, the effective average and marginal rates of consumption tax in any given year, for any income level, are far from clear. However, they can be obtained from the elasticity estimates, as shown below.

Consumption tax revenue elasticities require values for the parameters a and b. Benchmark values were chosen such that $a = 0.95$, with b calculated such that (for each year) a person with $z_i = 0$ has consumption, $m_i = ab$ equal to the value of the single person's income tax allowance. The Office of National Statistics, *Economic Trends* provides some data on the average proportion of disposable income consumed, which reveals figures between around 5 per cent and 12 per cent since 1989. Setting $m_i = ab$ equal to the single person's income tax allowance at $z_i = 0$ provides a convenient bench-mark because the single person's allowance is also the minimum income level recorded in the IRS income distribution database. However, the existence of social transfers could lead to consumption at very low income levels exceeding or falling short of this level. For example, FES data for most years suggest that, for the lowest income decile, average consumption expenditure marginally exceeds the upper income boundary for this group. Benchmark values of b used are shown in Table 5.8. Sensitivity to these values was also examined and is discussed below.

5.3.4 Consumption Tax Elasticity Estimates

Using equation (5.14) and the simulated distribution of 20,000 taxpayers used for examining the income tax revenue elasticities, consumption tax revenue elasticity estimates for each year were obtained, and are shown in Table 5.8, for all indirect taxes combined. It would be possible to apply these methods to examine tax revenue elasticities for individual consumption items, though this is not pursued here. Figure 5.5 compares the combined consumption tax revenue elasticities with those reported in subsection 5.2.4 for income taxes.

It can be seen from Figure 5.5 that the consumption tax revenue elasticity generally fell during the period, from around 0.8–0.9 in the early 1990s to about 0.7 by 2000. As expected, Figure 5.5 also reveals a tendency for the consumption tax elasticity to move inversely with the elasticity of income taxes. The more elastic are income tax revenues (mtr_i exceeds atr_i), the lower is the residual progression component of (5.14), and hence, *ceterus paribus*, the lower is the revenue elasticity of consumption taxes.

A comparison of columns 3 and 4 of Table 5.8 shows that ignoring additions to, and deductions from, net income (such as savings and transfers), by setting $b = 0$ and $a = 1$, has a substantial effect on consumption tax revenue elasticity estimates. The allowance for transfers and savings reduces the revenue elasticity to well below unity in each year, whereas failure to include a savings effect makes consumption tax revenues appear to be elastic in the

Table 5.8: Consumption Tax Revenue Elasticities

Year	b	Using current shares		Using 1993	Using 1993	$\eta_{R,Y}$
		$a = 0.95$	$a = 1$	1993	1993	
		b : as col. 2	$b = 0$	shares	shares	
1989	2932	0.854	1.078	0.774	0.854	1.091
1990	3163	0.853	1.109	0.752	0.822	1.117
1991	3468	0.882	1.141	0.755	0.823	1.120
1992	3626	0.757	1.020	0.747	0.814	1.093
1993	3626	0.745	1.006	0.745	0.812	1.105
1994	3626	0.712	0.946	0.729	0.795	1.108
1995	3711	0.690	0.924	0.730	0.796	1.098
1996	3963	0.712	0.953	0.733	0.802	1.090
1997	4258	0.717	0.952	0.723	0.799	1.099
1998	4416	0.724	0.971	0.735	0.808	1.099
1999	4563	0.712	0.959	0.731	0.805	1.087
2000	4616	0.714	0.957	0.733	0.807	1.102

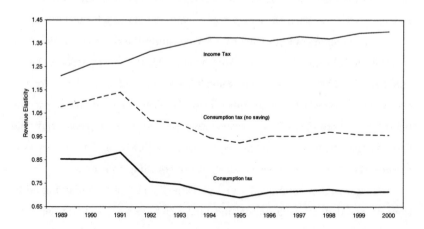

Figure 5.5: Consumption Tax Revenue Elasticities

early 1990s, and approximately proportional thereafter. The lower elasticity when $b = 0$ and $a = 1$ arises because the first term in (5.14) is unity, and the different levels of total expenditure for each individual imply different total expenditure elasticities of demand. However, the time–series pattern remains similar in the two cases.

The table also reveals that, when the income tax structure is relatively flat, as it became after the budget reforms of the mid–1980s, this generates an especially low income tax revenue elasticity, so that it is possible for the elasticity of consumption taxes to rise significantly. This appears to have happened in the late 1980s and early 1990s, when the consumption tax elasticity reached 1.14 in the no–savings case (or 0.9 in the savings case).

Allowing for alternative values of the consumption function parameters, a and b, around the benchmark case, suggests that revenue elasticity results are not especially sensitive to particular values. For example, in the benchmark case $b = £4563$ in 1999. Thus, with $a = 0.95$, consumption for those with zero disposable income equals the 1999 single person's allowance of £4335. Raising b by almost 10 per cent to £5000 or by over 30 per cent to £6000, reduces the consumption tax revenue elasticity by only 2.4 per cent or 7.6 per cent respectively. That is, the estimated elasticity of 0.712 in 1999 becomes 0.694 or 0.656 respectively. Also, reducing the value of a to 0.9, and raising b to £4817 for 1999 to maintain consumption at $z = 0$ equal to £4335, yields a revenue elasticity of 0.718. That is, reducing a by approximately 5 per cent increases the revenue elasticity by about 0.8 per cent.

5.3.5 The Impact of Budget–share Changes

The changes in the revenue elasticity of consumption taxes in Table 5.8 arise both from changes to fiscal parameters (income and consumption taxes) and from changes in consumers' budget shares. Some changes in consumers' spending patterns may arise from income growth while others may be partly

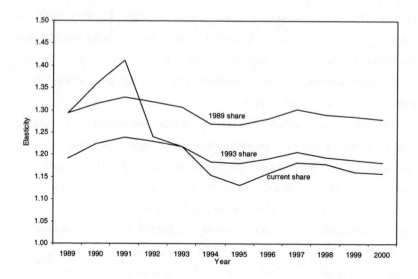

Figure 5.6: Decomposition of Consumption Tax Revenue Elasticities

in response to the fiscal changes. For example, the temporary reduction in expenditures on VAT–liable items in 1991 may have been partly in response to the tax rate increase to 17.5 per cent. There is also a longer–term trend towards a lower domestic fuel expenditure share following the introduction of VAT in 1994 (not shown in Figure 5.4).

Nevertheless it is interesting to compare the consumption tax revenue elasticity based on contemporary budget shares with those based on un-changed 1989 and 1993 budget shares; see Table 5.8 and Figure 5.6. From 1993, FES data are arranged by income deciles rather than the 16 income groups used previously. As a result, from 1993, comparisons using contem-poraneous and 1993–based budget shares are likely to be more accurate than those based on 1989 budget shares. The greater variation shown in column 3, which uses contemporary shares, indicates the importance of allowing for changes in consumption patterns over time. Fiscal changes, most of which relate to income taxation, also appear to have had a significant role, as is evident from changes in the elasticity values in columns 5 and 6 when budget shares are held constant.

The final column of Table 5.8 reports the elasticity of the combined income and consumption tax revenue, using current year budget shares and allowing for savings. This indicates that the generally declining values of the consumption tax revenue elasticity over time were approximately compensated by the rises in the income tax revenue elasticity. As a result the overall revenue elasticity was fairly constant, at around 1.09 to 1.10.

5.4   Individual Revenue Elasticities

Aggregate revenue elasticities are likely to be most useful for tax planning purposes, but individual elasticities can identify those taxpayers likely to experience the greatest change in tax liabilities as their incomes or fiscal parameters change. This section shows how revenue elasticities, marginal and average tax rates vary across income levels for specified individuals.

The familiar result that an individual's income tax revenue elasticity is simply the ratio of the marginal and average tax rates applies to any tax. Thus, for tax, T, the individual revenue elasticity is:

$$\eta_{T,y_i} = \frac{mtr_i}{atr_i} \tag{5.24}$$

where, as before, mtr_i and atr_i are the marginal and average tax rates faced by an individual with income y_i. Given the individual revenue elasticity values computed using the expression in (5.14), and given the value of the atr_i for consumption taxes, atr_{v_i}, the marginal consumption tax rate can therefore readily be obtained using (5.24).

Table 5.9 shows atr_i, mtr_i and elasticity values for both income and consumption taxes for specified individual income levels from £5,000 to £100,000, using 1999 fiscal parameters and budget shares. This shows the tendency for

Table 5.9: Individual Revenue Elasticities and Tax Rates

Annual Income	η_{T_y,y_i}	mtr_{y_i}	atr_{y_i}	η_{T_v,y_i}	mtr_{v_i}	atr_{v_i}	$atr^*_{v_i}$ $= T_{v_i}/m_i$
5,000	5.798	0.075	0.013	0.582	0.129	0.222	0.123
10,000	1.792	0.199	0.111	0.708	0.121	0.171	0.134
15,000	1.389	0.210	0.151	0.807	0.123	0.152	0.139
20,000	1.257	0.214	0.170	0.871	0.126	0.145	0.144
25,000	1.192	0.217	0.182	0.909	0.127	0.140	0.148
30,000	1.154	0.219	0.190	0.961	0.136	0.141	0.155
35,000	1.673	0.350	0.209	0.836	0.113	0.135	0.155
40,000	1.592	0.356	0.233	0.865	0.112	0.130	0.155
45,000	1.435	0.360	0.251	0.890	0.122	0.125	0.155
50,000	1.370	0.364	0.266	0.912	0.110	0.121	0.155
100,000	1.148	0.382	0.333	1.026	0.108	0.105	0.155

the income tax revenue elasticity to decline as income increases, but with step increases when incomes cross the relevant income tax thresholds, of £5835 and £32335 in 1999. The reverse is true for consumption taxes. The *mtrs* for income taxes are not simply the statutory 0.23 and 0.40 rates. They also reflect the effects of income–related deductions which reduce the effective marginal tax rate below the statutory rate at each income level. For consumption taxes, marginal and average rates both fall as income increases, with the marginal rate lying below the average rate.

Around mean income levels, approximately £18,200 in 1999, the *mtrs* and *atrs* of consumption taxes as a whole are approximately 12 per cent and 15 per cent respectively. At low incomes, consumption tax rates appear high (for example, $atr_{v_i} = 0.22$ at $y_i = 5000$), and generally decline with income levels. However, this reflects the calculation of tax rates from tax payments relative to earned incomes, y_i. Non–wage income and proportionately lower income tax payments give a relative boost to expenditures, and consumption tax payments, for such individuals. The relevant tax base for consumption taxes is total expenditure. It can be seen from the final column of Table 5.9 that average consumption tax rates, $atr^*_{v_i}$, calculated on this basis are

much lower at low incomes and rise slightly across income levels, to around
15 per cent at £30,000. It is this latter average tax rate which is relevant for
assessing the degree of progression of consumption taxes. These would appear
overall to be slightly progressive at incomes below £30,000, and proportional
thereafter (though these tax rates do not allow for indirect incidence effects
via taxation of inputs). Implicitly therefore, the tendency for higher income
individuals to spend proportionately more on VAT–liable items is partially
compensated by proportionately smaller expenditures on other taxed goods.

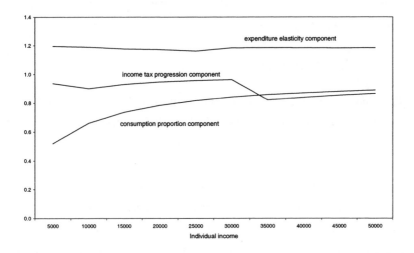

Figure 5.7: Components of the Consumption Tax Elasticity

Finally, Table 5.9 (column 5) shows that the individual consumption tax
revenue elasticity generally rises with income levels. It is useful to examine
how far this is due to differences in consumption patterns or income tax liabilities across income levels. Equation (5.14) showed that the consumption
tax revenue elasticity can be decomposed into three multiplicative components reflecting the proportion of disposable income consumed, the degree
of progression of the income tax, and the average expenditure elasticity of

taxed goods. This decomposition is shown in Figure 5.7. It can be seen that the expenditure elasticity (of taxed goods) component is approximately constant across income levels, despite a tendency for higher income individuals to consume more VAT–liable goods. The income tax progression component increases slightly with incomes except for discrete decreases immediately above marginal rate thresholds. Overall this component is smaller at relatively high, compared to low, income levels. It is clear therefore that the rising revenue elasticity is essentially due to the consumption proportion component. Indeed, this line, unlike the others in the figure, begins at 0 when $y = 0$, and therefore rises rapidly at low income levels.

5.5 Conclusions

This chapter has examined the revenue responsiveness properties of UK income and consumption taxes since the late 1980s using recently developed expressions for tax revenue elasticities. These allow elasticities to be derived in terms of relatively few parameters for which data are usually readily available. Annual income tax revenue elasticities were obtained for 1989–2000 using annual Inland Revenue income distribution data to estimate the parameters of a lognormal income distribution which is used to simulate a population, together with data on income tax rates, allowances and deductions.

The results revealed that an important component of the revenue elasticity – the income elasticity of income–related deductions – appears to be variable over time. It fell substantially with the limitation and then the withdrawal of mortgage interest tax relief. But it stabilised in the mid–1990s and has begun to increase again in recent years with the rise in private pension schemes.

Income tax revenue elasticity estimates, of around 1.3 to 1.4 in the early 1990s, are lower than those previously reported for the mid–1980s, reflecting in part the flattening of the income tax structure since that time. They are also more in line with the observed buoyancy of income taxes of around 1.09. This suggests that discretionary tax changes have, *ceteris paribus,* considerably reduced tax revenues, causing the tax elasticity substantially to exceed tax buoyancy, especially in the late 1990s. In addition, income tax revenue elasticities appear to be rising during the 1990s partly in response to the increased deductions referred to above, and the reversal of some of the 1980s tax reforms.

Elasticities for consumption taxes reveal interesting results. Since these taxes are often regarded as only mildly progressive, their elasticity has generally been presumed to be close to unity. This appears to be confirmed when consumers' savings and transfer payments are ignored. However, when the impacts on the consumption tax revenue elasticity of savings and transfers, the revenue responsiveness of income taxes, and changing consumption patterns towards tax–liable goods are recognised, values for the revenue elasticity of around 0.7 are obtained for recent years. These have generally fallen from around 0.9 in the early 1990s. With consumption tax buoyancy around 1.4 over this period, discretionary tax changes would appear to have substantially raised, rather than reduced, revenues in this case.

Chapter 6

Consumption Taxes in Australia

This chapter starts from the basic definition of a progressive consumption tax as one for which the marginal tax rate is greater than the average tax rate at all total expenditure levels. As previous chapters have shown, the ratio of the marginal rate to the average rate provides a measure of liability progression at the relevant income level, first proposed by Musgrave and Thin (1948). It also measures the revenue elasticity of the tax. This chapter considers the question of how redistributive it is possible to make consumption taxes, using a non–uniform set of rates, as measured by revenue elasticity.

In section 6.2, this progressivity measure is used to extend the simple view that a consumption tax is most progressive, or inequality–reducing, if it taxes most heavily those goods which form a systematically higher proportion of the budgets of high–income households. A neutral consumption tax, that is, having no redistributive effect, is achieved when a uniform rate is levied on *all* goods and services, since the real incomes of all households are reduced by the same proportion. Here, indirect taxes are judged in terms of their tax base, total expenditure, rather than income. Issues relating to the use of income in examining indirect taxes, and the role of savings, are discussed in other chapters and in Creedy (1998). Profiles of the variation in liability progression with total expenditure are examined for several indi-

135

rect tax structures in Australia along with alternative structures designed to introduce more redistribution.

In view of the limitations of liability progression as a distributional or welfare measure, section 6.3 then extends the analysis to consider welfare changes, measured in terms of Hicksian equivalent variations, at different total expenditure levels. In addition, social evaluations, based on the use of alternative social welfare functions which reflect distributional value judgements, are presented. Brief conclusions are drawn in section 6.4.

6.1   Consumption Taxes and Redistribution

It is sometimes suggested that indirect taxes provide a blunt instrument for redistribution; for example, see Stern (1990) and Chisholm *et al.* (1990, p.150). However, it is not easy to provide a simple measure of the redistributive potential of a general tax structure. Sah (1983), for example, focused on measuring improvements to the welfare of the worst–off individual, from a set of commodity taxes and subsidies (negative taxes), subject to the government budget constraint. He obtained an upper limit in terms of the maximum budget share of the worst–off person as a ratio of the minimum average budget share in the economy. However, this is of limited use where concern is with measures of tax progressivity or redistribution over the whole range of incomes. The issue is examined here by considering liability progression across a range of income levels, for various (including extreme) forms of indirect taxation, together with the wider implications for inequality and social welfare.

In the context of income taxation, it is in principle possible to specify a tax function, involving income and a range of non–income variables, that can achieve precisely the type of income redistribution required. The term redistribution is used, even if there are no explicit transfers, to describe the reduction in inequality from pre–tax to post–tax distributions. The fundamental limits to redistribution are imposed by labour supply incentive effects and population heterogeneity. But in practice, tax functions are specified in terms of a set of income thresholds, between which marginal tax rates are constant, and a limited range of non–income variables relating, for example, to household size and composition, which influence deductions. There are usually other endogenous, and often complex, deductions. Some errors (or deviations from the desired schedule) are therefore inevitable, and a practical income tax scheme is likely to have various unintended horizontal inequities that reduce the intended vertical redistribution.

A greater range of constraints is imposed on the ability of non–uniform consumption taxes to reduce the inequality of consumption, measured in terms of total expenditure minus the indirect tax paid. Indirect tax rates are by their nature set independently of individuals' income levels and the usual non–income characteristics used in specifying an income tax structure. One obvious limitation is that virtually all broad commodity groups are consumed by all types of household at all income levels. Thus, for example, the exemption of food from a general consumption tax benefits all income groups, while it is motivated by a desire to introduce progressivity. There are strong administrative constraints on the number of separate indirect tax rates that could be used. It may be possible to find certain luxury goods which are most likely to be consumed only by high–income households but, like extremely high marginal income tax rates at very high incomes, these are not likely to produce much revenue or have much overall impact on inequality. Differentiation by very narrow commodity groups or brand names would involve considerable administrative problems.

6.2 Liability Progression

This section examines the behaviour of the liability progression or revenue elasticity measure of progressivity, in the context of indirect taxation. The definitions and basic properties are presented in subsection 6.2.1. A crucial role is played by budget shares and their variation with household total expenditure. Such variations are examined using Australian Household Expenditure Survey data in subsection 6.2.2. Subsection 6.2.3 goes on to examine liability progression in Australia before and after the introduction of a goods and services tax in 2000. The subsection also considers hypothetical structures which are substantially more selective and redistributive.

6.2.1   Basic Properties

Let w_ℓ represent the budget share of the ℓth good, for $\ell = 1, ..., n$. If v_ℓ is the *ad valorem* tax–exclusive rate on good ℓ, the tax–inclusive rate is $v'_\ell = v_\ell / (1 + v_\ell)$ and the total consumption tax revenue paid by an individual i, T_{v_i}, with total expenditure of m_i, is given by

$$T_{v_i} = m_i \sum_{\ell=1}^{n} v'_\ell w_{i\ell} \qquad (6.1)$$

As noted above, the ratio of the marginal tax rate, dT_{v_i}/dm_i, to the average tax rate, T_{v_i}/m_i, is equivalent to the elasticity of tax revenue with respect to total expenditure, $\eta_{T_{v_i}, m_i} = (dT_{v_i}/T_{v_i}) / (dm_i/m_i)$. This provides an indication of the progressivity of the indirect tax system. From (6.1), the marginal rate, where i subscripts are dropped for convenience, is:

$$\frac{dT}{dm} = \sum_{\ell=1}^{n} v'_\ell w_\ell + m \sum_{\ell=1}^{n} v'_\ell \frac{dw_\ell}{dm} \qquad (6.2)$$

The revenue elasticity becomes:

$$\eta_{T,m} = 1 + \frac{\sum_{\ell=1}^{n} v'_\ell w_\ell \left(\frac{dw_\ell}{dm} \frac{m}{w_\ell} \right)}{\sum_{\ell=1}^{n} v'_\ell w_\ell} \qquad (6.3)$$

This can be expressed in terms of the total expenditure elasticities, e_ℓ. Given that $w_\ell = p_\ell q_\ell / m$, where p_ℓ and q_ℓ are the price and quantity of good ℓ, it can be seen that:

$$\frac{m}{w_\ell} \frac{dw_\ell}{dm} = \frac{m}{q_\ell} \frac{dq_\ell}{dm} - 1 = e_\ell - 1 \qquad (6.4)$$

Hence:

$$\eta_{T,m} = 1 + \frac{\sum_{\ell=1}^{n} v'_{\ell} w_{\ell} \left(e_{\ell} - 1 \right)}{\sum_{\ell=1}^{n} v'_{\ell} w_{\ell}} \qquad (6.5)$$

Using the adding–up conditions that $\sum_{\ell=1}^{n} w_{\ell} e_{\ell} = \sum_{\ell=1}^{n} w_{\ell} = 1$, (6.5) shows that $\eta_{T,m} = 1$ at all total expenditure levels when taxes are uniform, that is when all $v'_{\ell} = v'$. In chapter 3, the indirect tax revenue elasticity with respect to gross income, y, was shown to be $(1 - t_k) y \sum_{\ell=1}^{n} v'_{\ell} w_{\ell} e_{\ell} / \left(m \sum_{\ell=1}^{n} v'_{\ell} w_{\ell} \right)$, where t_k is the relevant marginal income tax rate. With a progressive income tax, this revenue elasticity is less than 1 for a uniform consumption tax system, unlike the elasticity with respect to expenditure considered above.

A tax structure is more progressive than another if it has higher values of $\eta_{T,m}$ at all m. The property of an increasing budget share is equivalent to $e_{\ell} > 1$. The above argument that, for progression, goods which form a higher proportion of the budgets of poorer households should be taxed at a lower rate translates into the statement that goods with total expenditure elasticities greater than 1 should be taxed most heavily. However, a degree of progressivity can be obtained even if taxes are imposed on some goods for which $e_{\ell} < 1$ at some income levels. In practice, taxes are likely to be imposed on some of these goods for non–distributional reasons, including merit good arguments and revenue requirements.

For any demand system, the total expenditure elasticities tend to unity as total expenditure increases, though this tendency may not be monotonic; hence $\eta_{T,m}$ tends to 1 as m tends to ∞, whatever the nature of the tax structure. For discussion of this property, see Deaton and Muellbauer (1980). A further implication of the convergence of the total expenditure elasticities towards unity is that, in those cases for which $e_{\ell} > 1$ at all levels of m, the elasticity declines as m increases, though again this may not necessarily be monotonic. This provides a further constraint on the progressivity of an indirect tax structure.

Consider a two–rate system in which goods are ordered such that the first s goods are taxed at a uniform rate. From (6.5) the revenue elasticity becomes:

$$\eta_{T,m} = \frac{\sum_s w_\ell e_\ell}{\sum_s w_\ell} \qquad (6.6)$$

Let $\eta_{w_\ell,m}$ denote the elasticity of the ℓth budget share with respect to total expenditure. Then (6.6) can be written as:

$$\eta_{T,m} = 1 + \frac{\sum_s w_\ell \eta_{w_\ell,m}}{\sum_s w_\ell} \qquad (6.7)$$

In this case the revenue elasticity is independent of the uniform rate imposed on taxed goods. The tax rate can therefore be set only in order to satisfy a revenue requirement. This independence of $\eta_{T,m}$ from the common indirect tax rate means that the government has only one policy variable, the value of s, with which to influence progression in such a system. This is a serious limitation on the ability to design a progressive consumption tax structure. An income tax with a single marginal rate above a tax–free threshold has, in comparison, considerable redistributive scope.

From equation (6.6), the revenue elasticity depends in a clear way on the extent to which the tax base changes as total expenditure increases. A similar result applies for an income tax system in which allowances are endogenous, whereby if allowances increase in the same proportion as income, the revenue elasticity is 1. In a multi–step income tax function, the revenue elasticity is independent of tax rates only for those in the first tax bracket; see chapter 2. Compared with an income tax system, for which the average tax rate at low incomes can be made very low by suitably setting the tax–free income threshold, it is much harder to impose an indirect tax structure that achieves a high revenue elasticity (liability progression) at low income levels. Furthermore, in a direct tax system, the marginal rate can easily be increased at higher income thresholds, enabling the liability progression to increase by discrete jumps, whereas indirect taxes are imposed on goods independently of the circumstances of purchasers.

The expression in (6.6) can be related to the earlier general suggestion that progression requires higher rates to be imposed on goods for which $e_\ell > 1$. In a system with uniform taxation on a selection of goods, liability progression is maximised (at a given total expenditure level) by taxing only the good with maximum $e_\ell > 1$. This requirement of extreme selectivity to achieve maximum progressivity is clearly not a practical policy option. The revenue requirement is likely to imply an unrealistically high tax rate. Furthermore, in practice the tax changes are likely to affect the budget shares, providing a further restriction on the ability to impose high tax rates. With a maximum feasible tax rate, other goods need to be taxed to satisfy a revenue requirement. In general, the rule for maximising progressivity is simply to start by ranking commodity groups in decreasing order of expenditure elasticity. Then start with the group having the highest expenditure elasticity, and add further groups as required in order to meet the revenue requirement, bearing in mind the practical constraints on the maximum tax rate that can be imposed on each group. In order for the revenue elasticity to exceed the corresponding value under a uniform tax on those goods subject to a non–zero rate, it is necessary to set $v_\ell > v_j$ where $e_\ell > e_j$.

If negative taxes, or subsidies, are allowed, it is possible to achieve substantially higher values of liability progression at lower levels of total expenditure. Furthermore, the imposition of negative taxes on some goods implies a progressivity maximising structure in which all goods are taxed, including those which have total expenditure elasticities less than 1 but are not subsidised. However, subsidies are typically not part of the consumption tax structures of industrialised countries. On the other hand, they are sometimes used for redistributive purposes in developing countries which rely on indirect taxes rather than having an income tax and transfer system.

6.2.2   Variations in Budget Shares

The empirical analysis of liability progression requires estimates of total expenditure elasticities, at a number of total expenditure levels, for a range of commodity groups. These elasticities can be obtained using cross–sectional survey data. However, the relationship between average budget shares and total household expenditure displays substantial variability. Hence the calculation of elasticities at alternative total expenditure levels, based on such shares, would result in a number of negative values and excessive variability. It is therefore useful to estimate the parameters of a specified functional form relating budget shares to total expenditure.

Let w_ℓ denote the average budget share of good ℓ for households with total expenditure of m. The results in Table 6.1 show that the following specification provides a good description of the variation in the budget shares:

$$w_\ell = a_\ell + b_\ell \ln(m) + \frac{c_\ell}{m} \qquad (6.8)$$

This has the added advantage that independent estimation for each commodity group has the property that predicted shares always add to unity. Eliminating the term in c_ℓ/m gives the form used in the 'almost ideal demand system' proposed by Deaton and Muellbauer (1980). The estimates are for each of the 14 commodity groups used in the Australian 1993 Household Expenditure Survey, where values of m are measured in cents per week. The results are for all households, with no adjustment made for size and composition.

Differentiating (6.8) gives:

$$\frac{dw_\ell}{dm} = \frac{b_\ell m - c_\ell}{m^2} \qquad (6.9)$$

so that w_ℓ unequivocally falls as m rises if $b_\ell < 0$ and $c_\ell > 0$; or if $c_\ell < 0$, so long as $m > c_\ell/b_\ell$. Hence the budget shares fall for Australian households over the relevant range of household total expenditure in the cases of: current housing costs; electricity, gas and other fuels; food and non–alcoholic

Table 6.1: Budget Shares: All Households Combined

Commodity Group	a_ℓ	b_ℓ	c_ℓ	$\overline{R}^2$
Current housing costs	0.8439	-0.0628	-311.4117	0.9603
Electricity, gas and other fuels	0.1688	-0.0130	328.4054	0.9874
Food and beverages	0.9671	-0.0697	-495.8344	0.9773
Spirits, beer and wine	0.1546	-0.0078	-431.7199	0.5450
Tobacco	0.2110	-0.0169	-335.5932	0.9281
Clothing and footwear	-0.0570	0.0096	-91.8081	0.8194
Furniture and appliances	-0.1774	0.0204	124.5691	0.8643
Postal and telephone charges	0.2572	-0.0185	64.6643	0.9580
Health services	0.2507	-0.0180	-395.9763	0.8101
Motor vehicles and parts	-0.0151	0.0153	-751.3042	0.8265
Recreational items	0.0937	0.0039	-826.4007	0.8096
Personal care products	0.0653	-0.0041	-67.4465	0.5269
Miscellaneous	-0.0782	0.0133	-200.5533	0.8326
House building payments	-1.6847	0.1514	3390.4360	0.8099

beverages; postal and telephone charges; health services; and personal care products. The above discussion has shown that any attempt to make the indirect tax structure as progressive as possible would therefore not tax these commodity groups.

Alternatively, the shares rise as total expenditure rises in the case of: clothing and footwear; furniture and appliances; motor vehicles and parts; recreational items; miscellaneous; and house building payments. These groups would therefore be taxed in any system attempting to introduce progressivity. In the cases of alcohol and tobacco the budget shares initially rise before falling in the higher total expenditure groups, so that the overall effects of taxes on these commodity groups are more ambiguous.

6.2.3 Alternative Tax Structures

This subsection examines the variation in revenue elasticities with total expenditure for a range of alternative tax structures, using the predicted budget shares obtained from the regression equations reported in the previous subsection. As mentioned above, the predicted budget shares always add to 1. However, they do not guarantee that all $w > 0$ at all total expenditure levels; a small number of minor adjustments were therefore made at the lower levels of m. First, the Australian indirect tax systems before and after the introduction of the goods and services tax (GST) are considered. This is followed by consideration of hypothetical cases.

Many indirect taxes operated in Australia before July 2000. These included wholesales sales tax, excise tax, financial institutions duty, payroll tax, land tax, stamp duties, municipal rates and primary production tax; see Johnson *et al.* (1997, pp. 14–17, 22–24) and Sood and Scutella (1997) for further details. The final effect of these taxes on consumer prices is the result of a complex process, particularly as different taxes are imposed at different stages of the production and distribution process and some taxes are unit taxes while others are *ad valorem*. The effective rates on different commodity groups depend on the extent to which taxes are shifted forward at each production stage and on the nature of inter–industry transactions.

Table 6.2: Effective Indirect Tax Rates

No.	Description	Pre–GST	GST–P	Post–GST
1	Current housing costs	0.1363	0.1791	0.1988
2	Fuel and power	0.0872	0.1634	0.1697
3	Food and Non–alcoholic Beverages	0.1142	0.1753	0.1015
4	Alcohol	0.2969	0.3332	0.3046
5	Tobacco products	0.6826	0.8959	0.9025
6	Clothing and footwear	0.0681	0.1476	0.1548
7	Furnishings and equipment	0.1072	0.1382	0.1493
8	Services and operation	0.0903	0.1176	0.1183
9	Medical care and health	0.0569	0.0362	0.0462
10	Transport	0.2381	0.1977	0.2039
11	Recreation and entertainment	0.1436	0.1930	0.1927
12	Personal care	0.1259	0.1360	0.1138
13	Miscellaneous goods and services	0.1411	0.1241	0.1566
14	Other capital housing	0.1147	0.1462	0.1622

Estimates of the effective indirect tax rates arising from the pre–GST system were reported by Johnson *et al.* (1999, p.12) for 14 commodity groups used by the Household Expenditure Survey. They also reported the price changes for the GST system that was initially proposed and which included the application of GST to food; this system is referred to here as GST–P. The effective rates are shown in Table 6.2. Johnson (1999) reported values to just one decimal point, but more detailed values were provided for use here. In addition, the rates are obtained after converting the price changes into tax rates, using the result that if the tax rate changes from v_1 to v_2, the price increase is given by $\dot{p} = (v_2 - v_1) / (1 + v_1)$, so that $v_2 = v_1 + (1 + v_1)\dot{p}$.

The GST that was eventually introduced involved several modifications to the proposals, the most important of which was the exemption of most food from the GST. The resulting post–GST indirect tax rates are shown in the final column of Table 6.2. These are the same as those used by Johnson *et al.* (1999). Potential general equilibrium effects of indirect taxes on factor prices were ignored in calculating these rates. For example, a tax imposed on a good which comprises a high proportion of total expenditure of low–wage households may involve, through output and factor substitution effects and depending on relative factor intensities, a compensating rise in the incomes of those households. The two sets of rates clearly do not generate the same amount of revenue from indirect taxes.

The values reported in the table are effective tax–exclusive *ad valorem* rates, calculated using the method devised by Scutella (1997). This involves tracing the incidence through the input–output matrix, assuming full shifting at each stage. It can be seen that there is a considerable degree of non–uniformity in the effective rates. In view of the large number of industries in the input–output matrix compared with the number of commodity groups in the HES, it was necessary to carry out a certain amount of consolidation. Hence the rates shown can only be regarded as approximate rates obtained under strong shifting assumptions.

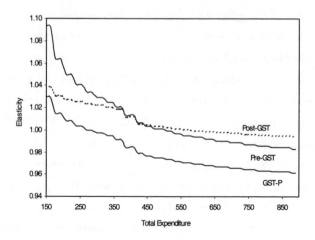

Figure 6.1: Elasticity Profiles for the Australian Tax Structure

Profiles of the revenue elasticity are shown in Figure 6.1. These profiles are not smooth because of the use of total expenditure groups (those used to obtain average budget shares for the regressions), within which the budget shares are assumed to be constant. It can be seen that the liability progression of the pre–GST system is slightly above 1 only for total expenditure levels below about $500 per week. For the GST–P structure, it falls below 1 after about $250 per week. The post–GST system is only slightly more progressive, at all total expenditure levels, than the initially proposed system that included a GST on food. While the post–GST system has lower values of liability progression at the lower total expenditure levels, these are closer to unity at the higher expenditure levels. However, the differences are small and the flatness of the profiles suggests that, despite the non–uniformity involved, their overall effect differs little from a uniform system. This was confirmed by examination of the Gini measure of inequality of total expenditure net of indirect taxation; these were found to be not statistically significantly different.

Table 6.3: Alternative Tax Structures

No.	Description	A	B	C
1	Current housing costs			0.25
2	Electricity, gas and other fuels			0.35
3	Food and beverages			0.45
4	Spirits, beer and wine			
5	Tobacco			
6	Clothing and footwear	0.30	0.30	
7	Furniture and appliances	0.30	0.30	
8	Postal and telephone charges			0.20
9	Health services			0.25
10	Motor vehicles and parts	0.30	0.40	
11	Recreational items	0.30	0.20	
12	Personal care products			0.20
13	Miscellaneous	0.30	0.20	
14	House building payments	0.30	0.40	

Consider alternative structures designed to produce a larger amount of redistribution. Based on the earlier discussion, the following analysis considers the hypothetical tax structures shown in Table 6.3. Instead of imposing the extreme structure based on taxing only the good with the highest total elasticity, cases A and B tax those goods whose budget shares rise with income, that is, have an elasticity greater than one. Case A has a uniform tax imposed on a selection of goods, so that liability progression does not actually depend on the rate used. Case B has relatively higher taxes imposed on those groups for which the shares increase relatively faster with income: motor vehicles and parts (category 10) and house building payments (category 14) have the highest tax rate of 40 per cent, while a lower rate is imposed on recreational items (category 11) and miscellaneous (category 13). These systems obviously have far more selectivity than has been suggested in practice. For contrast, case C has a regressive structure involving non–uniform taxes on a selection of goods, for which the budget shares fall as income rises.

The profiles of the revenue elasticities (liability progression) are shown in

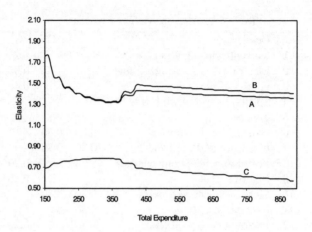

Figure 6.2: Elasticity Profiles for Alternative Tax Structures

Figure 6.2. Cases A and B are, as expected, quite similar, and give values that are higher than the actual tax structure at all the relevant total expenditure levels. Nevertheless, the highest elasticity values, at the lower total expenditure levels, are substantially below those achieved by a progressive income tax structure. The non–monotonic variation in the revenue elasticity arises because of the non–monotonic variations in the total expenditure elasticities as total expenditure varies. The profiles are also based on average budget shares within total expenditure groups. In practice the heterogeneity in consumption patterns between households with similar levels of total expenditure is likely to introduce horizontal inequities and reranking effects that militate against the attempt to increase redistribution.

6.3   Welfare Change Measures

The above discussion concentrated on local measures of tax progression. While this can be informative, it can be difficult to draw policy conclusions in cases where ambiguous outcomes arise, for example, where elasticity profiles such as those in Figure 6.1 cross. Revenue elasticities also cannot be used to measure overall effects on redistribution, or to evaluate the welfare implications of inequality or redistribution. This section therefore considers the effects of the alternative extreme indirect tax structures on measures of welfare change and on overall evaluations using a social welfare function. Estimation of demand responses and welfare changes present severe problems in Australia because of the paucity of data. Researchers do not have access to a time series of household expenditure data, and the available time series for consumption data are aggregative and cover relatively few commodity groups.

The results reported below make use of a result established by Frisch (1959) for directly additive utility functions, which relates own–price and cross–price elasticities to total expenditure elasticities, budget shares and the elasticity of the marginal utility of income (the Frisch parameter). There are well–known criticisms of the use of additivity; for example it does not allow for complements. The welfare changes are based on the linear expenditure system (LES), a special case of an additive utility function. In view of these strong assumptions, the results must be treated with caution.

The approach involves a set of price elasticities being computed for each of a range of total expenditure groups, following the general approach suggested in Creedy (1999), and described briefly in Appendix 6.1 below. Instead of using a single set of parameters, estimates of the LES are obtained for each of a number of total expenditure groups. Households within each group are assumed to have the same preferences, but these are allowed to vary between groups. If all households have identical tastes, additivity implies that optimal indirect tax rates are uniform. However, this does not arise in the present context because of the allowance for heterogeneity of expenditure patterns between groups. Equivalent variations are calculated for each of a range of total expenditure groups, using separate estimates of the linear expenditure function for each group. Price changes, $\dot{p}_\ell$, are regarded as arising from the indirect tax structure, so that $\dot{p}_\ell = v_\ell$.

Use is also made of a money metric welfare measure which, following King (1983), is often known as equivalent income. This is defined as the value of total expenditure, m_e, that, at some reference set of prices, p_r, gives the same utility as the actual total expenditure and prices. In terms of the indirect utility function, m_e is therefore defined by $V(p_r, m_e) = V(p, m)$. Using the expenditure function gives $m_e = E(p_r, V(p, m))$. Crucially, it is invariant with respect to monotonic variations in the utility function. When pre–change prices are used as reference prices, the change in equivalent income is the equivalent variation, so that equivalent income is given by $m_e = m - EV$, since pre–change equivalent income is simply m. The proportionate change in equivalent income following a set of price changes is EV/m. If this ratio is the same for all households, any relative measure of inequality of equivalent income is unchanged as a result of the tax change. The overall effects of a tax change can also be evaluated using a social welfare function specified in terms of equivalent incomes.

6.3.1   Equivalent Variations

The equivalent variations for the alternative tax structures, for a range of levels of weekly total expenditure (in dollars), are shown in Table 6.4. The median weekly total expenditure (in the Household Expenditure Survey) is $556; the lower and upper quartiles are $336 and $845; and the first and ninth deciles are $205 and $1227.

Under cases A and B it can be seen that the ratio, EV/m, increases as m increases, which is consistent with an inequality reducing effect. For a uniform system the ratio is constant. For example, with a uniform rate of $v_\ell = 0.15$ for all ℓ, then $\dot{p}_\ell = \dot{p} = 0.15$ for all ℓ, and $EV/m = \dot{p}/(1 + \dot{p}) = 0.13$ for all values of m. For B, the ratio EV/m increases more rapidly as m increases, but this difference is very small. Structure C gives rise, as

Table 6.4: Ratio of Equivalent Variations to Total Expenditure

m	A	B	C
200	0.078	0.075	0.189
400	0.102	0.098	0.163
600	0.118	0.116	0.146
800	0.129	0.128	0.133
1000	0.138	0.138	0.123
1200	0.145	0.147	0.115
1400	0.157	0.160	0.100

expected, to a reduction in EV/m as m increases, consistent with an increase in inequality.

6.3.2 Abbreviated Social Welfare Functions

An overall evaluation of a tax change can be made using a social welfare or evaluation function expressed in terms of the distribution of equivalent incomes. The abbreviated social welfare function associated with Atkinson's inequality measure is given by:

$$W_A = \overline{m}_e \left(1 - A\left(\varepsilon\right)\right) \tag{6.10}$$

where W_A is welfare per person, ε is the degree of constant relative inequality aversion, $\overline{m}_e$ is the arithmetic mean equivalent income and $A\left(\varepsilon\right)$ is Atkinson's inequality measure. This form means that a 1 per cent increase in equality is viewed as being equivalent to a 1 per cent increase in mean income, bearing in mind that the measure of equality increase depends on the value of ε. The expression for the abbreviated welfare function also gives the 'equally distributed equivalent income'; the use of the term 'equivalent' in this context should not be confused with the money metric concept of equivalent income. The same form of welfare function can be used with the Gini inequality measure (or the extended Gini, $G\left(s\right)$, for $s \geq 1$). The extended Gini is $G(s) = -\left(s/\overline{m}\right) \text{Cov}\{m, \left(1 - F(m)\right)^{s-1}\}$, where F denotes the distribution

Table 6.5: Household Groups

No.	Household type	number
1	All households	7590
2	Couple: no children	1430
3	Couple: no children, ≥ 1 retired	450
4	Couple: 1 dependant child	586
5	Couple: 2 dependant children	790
6	Couple: ≥ 3 dependant children	540
7	1 parent: 1 dependant child	190
8	1 parent: ≥ 2 dependant children	187
9	Single person, not retired	1000
10	Single person, retired	620

function, and the standard Gini is $G(2)$. On abbreviated welfare functions, see Lambert (1993).

The approach adopted here is to evaluate alternative welfare functions specified in terms of the distribution of equivalent income per equivalent adult, using a very simple adjustment, whereby the first adult is given a weight of 1, the second adult is given a weight of 0.6 and each child is given a weight of 0.3. See Johnson *et al.* (1995) for discussion of alternative scales used in Australia. Households were divided into 9 separate groups, described in Table 6.5. These groups cover about 75 per cent of all households in the Household Expenditure Survey. For groups 2 to 10, the number of equivalent adults were set respectively to [1.6, 1.6, 1.9, 2.2, 2.6, 1.3, 1.7, 1, 1]. In computing the welfare effects, separate elasticities and parameters of the utility functions were obtained for each household type and total expenditure level.

Values of inequality and social welfare, based on equivalent incomes per equivalent adult, are shown in Table 6.6. These are compared with a uniform structure that has no redistributive effect. The uniform tax rate was set at 0.15, which is approximately revenue neutral. It can be seen that structures

Table 6.6: Equivalent Income per Equivalent Adult

ε	W_A	$A(\varepsilon)$	v	$G(v)$	W_G
Uniform taxes					
0.10	562.08	0.0212	1.10	0.0646	537.17
1.60	394.33	0.3133	2.60	0.4472	317.48
Tax structure A					
0.10	562.95	0.0195	1.10	0.0615	538.84
1.60	406.59	0.2919	2.60	0.4313	326.54
Tax structure B					
0.10	563.01	0.0193	1.10	0.0611	539.03
1.60	407.57	0.2901	2.60	0.4295	327.52

A and B give rise to lower values of inequality and higher social welfare. The inequality reduction therefore outweighs the reduction in average equivalent income per equivalent adult as the tax becomes more progressive. However, for all degrees of inequality aversion, the reduction in inequality is small, considering the substantial differences between the tax structures.

6.4 Conclusions

This chapter has examined the question of the extent to which redistribution can be achieved using a structure of consumption taxes with differential rates and exemptions. Although redistribution can be achieved by taxing most heavily those goods for which the income elasticity exceeds unity, for which the budget shares increase as income increases, there are strong limitations in view of the fact that virtually all households consume some goods in each commodity group (given a broad classification) and elasticities ultimately tend to unity as income rises.

The issue was examined by considering a local measure of progression, that of liability progression which is equivalent to the revenue elasticity with respect to total expenditure. Progressivity was found to be maximised when only one commodity group, that having the largest total expenditure elasticity, is taxed. Where further commodity groups need to be taxed to meet revenue requirements, the tax rate should fall as the total expenditure elasticity falls. With a uniform structure, where some goods are exempt from a consumption tax, the liability progression is independent of the level of the tax rate.

The Australian indirect tax structure was examined along with alternative forms involving the taxation of only those groups for which the expenditure elasticity exceeds unity at all total expenditure levels. Budget shares and income elasticities were based on the Australian Household Expenditure Survey. In addition, comparisons were made of equivalent variations, for a range of levels of total expenditure, resulting from the imposition of indirect taxes. Inequality measures of the distribution of household equivalent income (a money metric welfare measure) per equivalent adult were computed. It was found that even extreme forms of differentiation in indirect taxes have a relatively small effect on liability progression and inequality. The results confirm the initial suggestion that consumption taxes provide only a blunt redistributive instrument.

Appendix 6.1: Utility, Demand Elasticities and Welfare

This appendix describes the method used to obtain demand elasticities and welfare changes using the linear expenditure system (LES), applied separately for a range of demographic groups, though the following notation generally omits the additional subscript.

The first stage is to obtain, for each household type, a set of average budget shares, $w_{k\ell}$, for each consumption category, ℓ, and a range of total expenditure groups, k. The total expenditure elasticities are obtained using the variations in budget shares for each commodity group. These were smoothed using predicted values from ordinary least squares regressions of the form:

$$w_{k\ell} = a_\ell + b_\ell \ln m_k + c_\ell \left(1/m_k\right) \tag{6.11}$$

for each commodity group (and household type), where the values of m_k correspond to the arithmetic mean values of total expenditure in each group, k.

The second stage is to compute own–price and cross–price elasticities, $e_{\ell\ell}$ and $e_{\ell j}$ (again for each total expenditure group and household type) using Frisch's (1959) results for additive demand systems. The expressions require the use of the elasticity of the marginal utility of total expenditure with respect to total expenditure, ξ, often referred to as the Frisch parameter. If $\delta_{\ell j}$ denotes the Kroneker delta, such that $\delta_{\ell j} = 0$ when $\ell \neq j$, and $\delta_{\ell j} = 1$ when $\ell = j$, Frisch showed that the elasticities can be written as:

$$e_{\ell j} = -e_\ell w_j \left(1 + \frac{e_j}{\xi}\right) + \frac{e_\ell \delta_{\ell j}}{\xi} \tag{6.12}$$

It is necessary to make use of extraneous information about the way in which the Frisch parameter varies with total expenditure. A flexible specification, which extends the logarithmic form used by Lluch et al. (1977), for the variation in ξ_k with m_k is given by:

$$\ln\left(-\xi_k\right) = \phi - \alpha \ln\left(m_k + \theta\right) \tag{6.13}$$

By a process of trial and error, values of 9.2, 1.05 and 177 respectively for ϕ, α and θ were found to produce appropriate values of ξ. Alternative values, giving relatively steep and flat profiles, were used but the main results were found to be similar to those reported above.

The third stage involves obtaining parameters of the LES direct utility function (again for each total expenditure group and household type):

$$U = \prod_\ell \left(x_\ell - \gamma_\ell\right)^{\beta_\ell} \tag{6.14}$$

with $0 \leq \beta_\ell \leq 1$; x_ℓ and γ_ℓ are respectively the total consumption and committed consumption of good ℓ, and $\sum \beta_\ell = 1$. The own–price elasticity, $e_{\ell\ell}$, is given by:

$$e_{\ell\ell} = \frac{\gamma_\ell\left(1 - \beta_\ell\right)}{x_\ell} - 1 \tag{6.15}$$

The total expenditure elasticity of good ℓ, e_ℓ, is:

$$e_\ell = \frac{\beta_\ell m}{p_\ell x_\ell} \tag{6.16}$$

Having obtained the total expenditure elasticities from the smoothed budget shares, the corresponding values of β_ℓ at each total expenditure level were obtained using (6.16), whereby $\beta_\ell = e_\ell w_\ell$. Using the values of own–price elasticities as described in the second stage above, equation (6.15) can be used to solve for $p_\ell \gamma_\ell$, the committed expenditures for each good.

Defining the terms A and B respectively as $\sum_\ell p_\ell \gamma_\ell$ and $\prod \left(p_\ell/\beta_\ell\right)^{\beta_\ell}$, and omitting subscripts relating to total expenditure, the indirect utility function for the LES, $V(p, m)$, is:

$$V = \left(m - A\right)/B \tag{6.17}$$

The expenditure function, $E\left(p, U\right)$, the minimum expenditure required to achieve U at prices p, is found by inverting (6.17) and substituting E for m

to get:

$$E(p, U) = A + BU \tag{6.18}$$

If the vector of prices changes from p_0 to p_1, the equivalent variation, EV, is $EV = E(p_1, U_1) - E(p_0, U_1)$. Substituting for E using (6.18) gives:

$$EV = m - (A_0 + B_0 U_1) \tag{6.19}$$

Substituting for U_1, using equation (6.17) into (6.19) and rearranging gives:

$$EV = m - A_0 \left[1 + \frac{B_0}{B_1} \left(\frac{m}{A_0} - \frac{A_1}{A_0} \right) \right] \tag{6.20}$$

The term A_1/A_0 is a Laspeyres type of price index, using γ_ℓs as weights. The term B_1/B_0 simplifies to $\prod (p_{1\ell}/p_{0\ell})^{\beta_\ell}$, which is a weighted geometric mean of price relatives. These two terms can be expressed in terms of the $\dot{p}$s, since $p_{1\ell} = p_{0\ell}(1 + \dot{p}_\ell)$, and defining $s_\ell = p_{0\ell}\gamma_\ell / \sum_\ell p_{0\ell}\gamma_\ell$, it can be shown that $A_1/A_0 = 1 + \sum_\ell s_\ell \dot{p}_\ell$ and $B_1/B_0 = \prod_\ell (1 + \dot{p}_\ell)^{\beta_\ell}$. If all prices change by the same proportion, $\dot{p}_\ell = \dot{p}$ for all ℓ, and (6.20) becomes $EV/m = (1 - B_0/B_1) + (A_0/m)\{(B_0/B_1)(A_1/A_0) - 1\}$, with $B_1/B_0 = A_1/A_0 = 1 + \dot{p}$.

Equivalent income, following King (1983), is the value, m_e, which, at some reference set of prices, p_r, gives the same utility as the actual income level. In this context, income and total expenditure are synonymous. Hence m_e is defined by $V(p_r, m_e) = V(p, m)$. Using the expenditure function gives:

$$m_e = E(p_r, V(p, m)) \tag{6.21}$$

For the linear expenditure system, this gives:

$$m_e = \sum_\ell p_{r\ell}\gamma_\ell + \left\{ \prod_\ell \left(\frac{p_{r\ell}}{p_\ell} \right)^{\beta_\ell} \right\} \left\{ m - \sum_j p_j \gamma_j \right\} \tag{6.22}$$

If pre–change prices are used as reference prices, so that $p_{r\ell} = p_{0\ell}$ for all ℓ, the post–change equivalent income is the value of actual income (total expenditure) after the change less the equivalent variation; that is, $m_{1e} =$

$m_1 - EV$. In general the equivalent income function is not guaranteed to be concave, leading to the problem that its use in a social welfare function could lead the latter to favour disequalising transfers. Blackorby and Donaldson (1988) showed that concavity requires quasi–homotheticity. This assumption is satisfied by the LES. Homothetic utility functions are positive monotonic transformations of linear homogeneous utility functions for which $U(\theta x) = \theta U(x)$.

Chapter 7

Tax Revenue in New Zealand

This chapter provides estimates of the built–in flexibility of income and consumption taxes (GST and excise taxes) in New Zealand. As in previous chapters, the measure used is the revenue elasticity, for which values at individual and aggregate levels are reported. Detailed official forecasts of tax revenues in New Zealand are of course frequently made, though for various reasons these do not always involve the explicit calculation of revenue elasticities. Few independent estimates for New Zealand appear to have been published. However, various elasticities are given by van den Noord (2000, p. 19) for OECD countries, who reports elasticities of personal and indirect taxes, with respect to changes in GDP, of 1.2 for both sets of taxes in New Zealand. The elasticities reported here suggest that the value of 1.2 for indirect taxes (which appears to be based on regression analysis) is unrealistically high. The methods used in this chapter also allow the various influences on the size of New Zealand tax revenue elasticities to be identified, including the specific contributions of such excises as those on fuel, alcohol and tobacco.

The chapter is organised as follows. Section 7.1 first briefly reviews the relevant conceptual expressions for income and consumption tax revenue elasticities at the individual level, with some estimates based on the 2001 New Zealand tax structure in subsection 7.1.1. Section 7.2 then reports empirical estimates for aggregate revenue elasticities. These estimates use the standard assumption that all incomes increase by the same proportion from year to year. Subsection 7.2.2 models the more realistic case of non–equiproportional income changes. The computation of aggregate elasticities requires information about the distribution of taxable income. One approach to income tax revenue forecasting is to use a purely numerical approach based on a large sample survey, or (preferably) longitudinal data on consecutive years, of taxable income. However, an advantage of the present modelling approach is that it provides an understanding of the determinants of revenue elasticities. In addition, it requires only limited data which are available to all researchers: there are severe restrictions in New Zealand on access to individual data. It is then possible to examine the sensitivity of, say, income tax revenue elasticities to changes in the dynamic process of income changes from year to year, or the effects on consumption tax revenue elasticities of changes in expenditure patterns. Section 7.3 draws some brief conclusions.

7.1 Individual Revenue Elasticities

This section examines income tax revenue elasticities for individuals. The variation in individual elasticities with income provides a useful independent indication of the local progressivity of the tax structure, and of course the individual elasticities provide the basic components on which aggregate values are based. The appropriate formulae have been derived in previous chapters and need not be repeated here. The basic formula for the income tax revenue elasticity was shown in chapter 2 to be:

$$\eta_{T_y, y_i} = 1 + \left(\frac{a'_k}{y_i - a'_k} \right) \left(1 - \eta_{a'_k, y_i} \right) \tag{7.1}$$

where there are income–related allowances. For example, in the UK, where there is (or has been) tax relief for mortgage interest payments or pension contributions, it is necessary to introduce the concept of the income elasticity of effective thresholds, $\eta_{a'_k, y_i}$. The result in (7.1) then shows that the individual revenue elasticity must exceed unity if $\eta_{a'_k, y_i} < 1$. A positive value of $\eta_{a'_k, y_i}$ can be expected, but it is unlikely to exceed unity. For the UK case examined in chapter 5, it was found above that $\eta_{a'_k, y_i}$ takes values around 0.4, but varies significantly over time in response to changes in the tax deductibility of various income–related reliefs such as those for families, pensions and mortgages. However, in New Zealand there are virtually no deductions or allowances. Hence the set of tax thresholds does not change with individuals' incomes, and it is appropriate to set $\eta_{a'_k, y_i} = 0$ in (7.1), which simplifies the individual income tax revenue elasticity to:

$$\eta_{T_y, y_i} = \frac{y_i}{y_i - a'_k} \qquad (7.2)$$

For an individual, the revenue elasticity for all consumption taxes combined was derived in chapter 3. In some cases it is of interest to know the revenue elasticities for separate consumption goods, such as those for alcohol or tobacco. Using the same methodology as that adopted in previous chapters for all consumption goods, it is readily shown that there is an analogous revenue elasticity for individual goods, that is, $\eta_{T_{v\ell}, y_i}$. As in previous chapters, define z_i as individual i's net income, and γ_i as the fraction of z_i consumed, the consumption tax paid by person i on good ℓ can be written as:

$$T_{v\ell, i} = v'_\ell w_{i\ell} m_i = v'_\ell w_{i\ell} \gamma_i z_i \qquad (7.3)$$

where v'_ℓ is the tax–inclusive *ad valorem* indirect tax rate imposed on the ℓth good (for $\ell = 1, ..., n$), and $w_{i\ell}$ is person i's budget share of the ℓth good.

Writing $m_{i\ell} = w_{i\ell} m_i$ as expenditure on the ith good, the following relationships are easily obtained:

$$
\begin{aligned}
m_{i\ell} = w_{i\ell} m_i \quad &\text{implies:} \quad \eta_{m_{i\ell}, m} = 1 + \eta_{w_{i\ell}, m_i} \\
m_i = \gamma_i z_i \quad &\text{implies:} \quad \eta_{m_i, z_i} = 1 + \eta_{\gamma_i, z_i} \\
T_{v_{i\ell}} = v'_\ell m_{i\ell} \quad &\text{implies:} \quad \eta_{T_{v_{i\ell}}, m_{i\ell}} = 1
\end{aligned}
\qquad (7.4)
$$

Differentiating (7.3) with respect to income, y_i, and using the relationships in (7.4), it can be shown that:

$$\eta_{T_{v_\ell}, y_i} = \left(1 + \eta_{w_{i\ell}, m_i}\right)\left(1 + \eta_{\gamma_i, z_i}\right)\eta_{z_i, y_i} \tag{7.5}$$

where η_{z_i, y_i} is the elasticity of disposable income, z_i, with respect to y_i. Three elasticities appear on the right–hand side of (7.5). The first term in parentheses on the right–hand side of (7.5) can be expressed in terms of $e_{i\ell}$, the total expenditure elasticity of demand for the ℓth good by person i, since:

$$e_{i\ell} = 1 + \eta_{w_{i\ell}, m_i} \tag{7.6}$$

The last term in (7.5), η_{z_i, y_i}, is the familiar measure of residual progression, written as:

$$\eta_{z_i, y_i} = \eta_{(y_i - T_{y_i}), y_i} = \frac{1 - mtr_{y_i}}{1 - atr_{y_i}} \tag{7.7}$$

such that, combining (7.5), (7.6) and (7.7), it follows that:

$$\eta_{T_{v_\ell}, y_i} = e_{i\ell}\left(1 + \eta_{\gamma_i, z_i}\right)\left(\frac{1 - mtr_{y_i}}{1 - atr_{y_i}}\right) \tag{7.8}$$

This may be compared with the revenue elasticity for all consumption goods combined, derived in chapter 3 as:

$$\eta_{T_v, y_i} = \left(1 + \eta_{\gamma_i, z_i}\right)\left(\frac{1 - mtr_{y_i}}{1 - atr_{y_i}}\right)\left\{\sum_{\ell=1}^{n}\left(\frac{T_{i\ell}}{T_{v_i}}\right)e_{i\ell}\right\} \tag{7.9}$$

The only difference between (7.8) and (7.9), is the tax–share weighting of expenditure elasticities in (7.9). To calculate the weighted elasticity, it is necessary to distinguish only between goods facing different *ad valorum* tax rates. Hence, as for the combined goods case, the consumption tax revenue elasticity for good ℓ can be decomposed into three terms, reflecting the total expenditure elasticity for good ℓ, the way in which the proportion of disposable income consumed by i changes with income, and the degree of residual progression determined by individual i's marginal and average income tax rates.

In both (7.8) and (7.9) it is necessary to measure the elasticity of the consumption proportion with respect to income, η_{γ_i,z_i}, which may vary with incomes if savings rates vary across disposable income levels. For the UK case, the analysis in chapter 5 allowed for the possibility of a non–proportional relationship by using the specification:

$$m_i = a\left(z_i + b\right) \tag{7.10}$$

where 'over–spending' at low income levels can be viewed in terms of the existence of transfer payments and/or consumption out of savings. For this case, it can be shown that $1 + \eta_{\gamma_i,z_i}$ in (7.9) is equal to $z/\left(z + b\right)$ or, alternatively, $(1 - ab/m_i)$.

For the UK case examined in chapter 5, annual changes in revenue elasticities were of interest, so that it was appropriate to allow for a non–proportional savings relationship. For the New Zealand case considered here, however, the primary focus is on the response of tax revenues to income growth over the long–run (from the values observed in 2001). While a non–proportional relationship is generally accepted for cross–sectional income differences and, to a lesser extent, for time–series changes over the short–term, changes in the consumption proportion over the long–run are probably best regarded as proportional. The elasticity estimates below therefore allow for both proportional and non–proportional cases; for a proportional consumption function (including zero savings, where $a = 1$), $b = 0$, and hence in (7.9), $1 + \eta_{\gamma_i,z_i} = 1$.

7.1.1 Estimates of Individual Revenue Elasticities

This subsection shows how individual revenue elasticities can be expected to vary across income levels in New Zealand. The New Zealand income tax structure in 2001 has marginal tax rates of 0.15, 0.21, 0.33 and 0.39 applying above income thresholds of (NZ\$) 0, 9500, 38000, and 60000. There is thus no initial tax–free allowance. These are the effective rates and thresholds used

Table 7.1: Consumption Tax Rates (Percentages)

Commodity Group	Effective Tax Rate	Budget Share (at income = NZ$30,000)	Tax Share
GST only	12.5	64	57
Rent	0	12	0
Overseas travel	0	3	0
Road vehicles	7.05	4	2
Vehicle ownership expenses (mainly fuel)	58.64	7	21
Recreational vehicles	6.25	0	0
Tobacco	239.85	2	10
Alcohol	46.82	2	5
Financial/legal services	6.25	4	2
Expenditure n.e.c.	23.0	2	3

to calculate effective allowances, a'_k, allowing for the existence of the Low–Income Rebate since, as noted above, there are no income–related deductions in New Zealand.

Consumption tax revenue elasticity calculations require estimates of the *ad valorum*–equivalent indirect tax rates. Most goods are taxed at the 12.5 per cent Goods and Services Tax (GST) rate. However some expenditures, such as rent and overseas travel, are exempt from GST. Furthermore a number of excise taxes produce very different effective tax rates on goods such as fuel, alcohol and tobacco. The consumption tax rates used, together with the budget and tax shares of the main commodity groups (for an individual with annual income of approximately NZ$30,000), are given in Table 7.1. For details on the computation of these rates, see Young (2002). Table 7.1 confirms the dominance, in terms of budget or tax shares, of goods only liable to the 12.5 per cent GST rate, but also shows that fuel, tobacco and alcohol account for around 11 per cent of the spending (and over 35 per cent of the consumption tax paid) by an individual with an income of NZ$30,000, which is a little above the arithmetic mean income level.

It is necessary to have information about the total expenditure elasticities, at different expenditure levels, of the relevant commodity groups. However, it is not possible even if separate income–unit data from budget studies were available, to produce precise individual values since estimates must be based on the cross–sectional variation in budget shares as total expenditure varies. Also, as noted above, cross–sectional variations in expenditure may not necessarily reflect the adjustments to total expenditure changes that would take place over time. The question therefore arises of the level of disaggregation to be used. The estimates reported here are based on an overall distribution of taxable income and use published budget–share data derived from average expenditures for a range of goods and income groups, from the 2000–2001 Household Economic Survey (HES); further details of the method used are discussed in Appendix 7.1. These are for all households combined, rather than considering different household types separately; however, the methods could be applied to more disagreggated data, where available.

Finally, consumption function parameters, a and b in (7.10) are required. These are necessary even if a proportional consumption function is assumed since, though they do not affect the consumption tax revenue elasticity in this case, they do affect the total (income–plus–consumption) tax revenue elasticity via tax share weights (see chapter 2). In view of the considerable difficulty in obtaining reliable information about savings functions, three consumption function cases were examined. These are: the no savings case with $a = 1$, $b = 0$, the proportional savings case where $a = 0.95$, $b = 0$, and the non–proportional case with $a = 0.85$, $b = 3000$. The proportional case assumes that 95 per cent of disposable income is spent, while the non–proportional case implies an average propensity to consume out of disposable income of 0.95 at NZ$30,000.

Figure 7.1 shows how the income and consumption tax revenue elasticities (all goods) vary across income levels. This displays the standard property whereby the income tax elasticity generally declines as income rises, with discrete jumps taking place as individuals cross the tax thresholds, reflecting

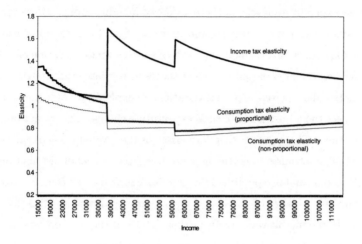

Figure 7.1: Individual Tax Revenue Elasticities

the sharp increase in the marginal rate of income tax.

For the consumption tax elasticity, two examples of the proportional and non–proportional cases are shown. As shown in equation (7.9), the shapes of these profiles reflect the three combined effects of the progressivity of the income tax, saving habits and differing expenditure elasticities across goods, combined with their associated *ad valorem* rates. Income tax progressivity tends to induce a 'mirror image' effect in the consumption tax profile via changes in disposable incomes. For example, discrete declines are evident in the consumption tax elasticity profiles in Figure 7.1 at the income tax thresholds and elasticities tend to rise at higher income levels.

However, at lower income levels consumption tax revenue elasticities also decline, rather than showing a mirror image of the decline in the income tax elasticity. This arises because of the dominant effect of declines in the tax–share weighted expenditure elasticities. These elasticities are shown in Figure 7.2, which reveals substantial declines in tax–share weighted expen-

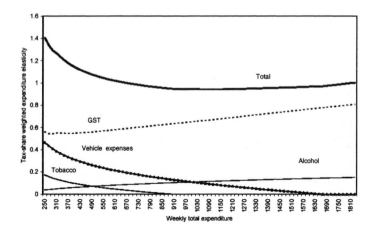

Figure 7.2: Tax-share Weighted Total Expenditure Elasticities

diture elasticities for vehicle ownership expenses (mainly fuel) and tobacco as incomes increase from relatively low levels. Since these expenditures face especially high tax rates, changes in these tax–share weighted elasticities dominate changes in the weighted average at low income levels. Figure 7.1 also reveals that the elasticities produced by the non–proportional consumption function relationship are generally slightly lower, by about 0.1 to 0.2 percentage points, than the proportional equivalents.

Revenue elasticities for the eight groups of commodities in Table 7.1 which contribute to consumption tax revenues can also be estimated using equation (7.8) above, and where a proportional consumption function is assumed; that is $\eta_{\gamma_i,z_i} = 0$. The main consumption groups of interest, in terms of their importance within individuals' budgets or tax payments, are goods taxed at the standard (12.5 per cent) GST rate, fuel, alcohol and tobacco. Figure 7.3 shows the relevant revenue elasticities, for a range of individual incomes.

It can be seen that, at around mean income levels of NZ$30,000, these revenue elasticities are bunched around unity, except for fuel (about 1.5)

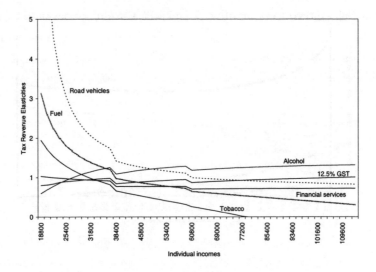

Figure 7.3: Revenue Elasticities for Consumption Goods

and road vehicle spending (over 2.0). Each consumption good elasticity profile reveals a discrete drop at the income tax thresholds (NZ$38,000 and
NZ$60,000) reflecting the impact of the residual progression component of
the elasticity expression in equation (7.8). At higher incomes, each profile is
relatively flat, with the exception of that for tobacco, which declines to a zero
elasticity at incomes over about NZ$80,000. This arises from the declining
budget share for tobacco at relatively high income levels. At higher income
levels only the revenue elasticity for alcohol appears to exceed unity. The
revenue elasticity for standard rate GST goods, the dominant contributor
to consumption tax revenues, can also be seen to be fairly constant across
incomes levels, at values around, or below, unity.

7.2 Aggregate Revenue Elasticities

This section examines aggregate tax revenue elasticities, which are the most relevant from the point of view of tax forecasting and planning, along with possible automatic stabilisation properties of the tax structure. Subsection 7.2.1 reports results for New Zealand in the case of equiproportional income changes. The implications of non–equiproportional income changes are then examined in subsection 7.2.2.

7.2.1 Estimates of Aggregate Revenue Elasticities

As previous chapters have demonstrated, aggregate revenue elasticities can readily be expressed as tax–share weighted sums of the relevant individual elasticities. Evaluation of these aggregate elasticities therefore requires, in addition to information about the income distribution (for computation of individuals' income and consumption tax shares), knowledge of the extent to which individuals' incomes change when aggregate income changes. A typical simplifying assumption is that all incomes increase by the same proportion, so that the elasticity of individual incomes with respect to aggregate income, $\eta_{y_i,Y} = 1$ and the aggregate income rax revenue elasticity is a simple tax–share weighted average of individual values. Furthermore, since total revenue is $T = T_Y + T_V$, the elasticity of total revenue with respect to aggregate income can be found as a tax–share weighted average of the income and consumption tax revenue elasticities. This subsection examines how aggregate revenue elasticities vary with aggregate income levels in New Zealand, under the assumption of equiproportional income changes.

As mentioned at the beginning of this chapter, an alternative approach would be to use detailed information, in the form of a large data set containing data on individual taxable incomes. Some studies use this entirely numerical approach, by imposing small income increases on each individual in the data set and examining the resulting tax changes, rather than using explicit formulae. Since such individual data are available only to a highly restricted group of users in New Zealand, the method used here is to parameterise the distribution, based on grouped income distribution data, and then to produce a simulated distribution of incomes by taking random draws from the fitted distribution.

Figure 7.6 in Appendix 7.1 shows the New Zealand grouped income distribution in 2001, and discusses the application of a lognormal distribution to summarise the data. It was found that a mean and variance of the logarithms of incomes of $\mu = 9.85$ and $\sigma^2 = 0.7$ provide a reasonable approximation to parameterise a lognormal income distribution. These values imply an arithmetic mean income of 26,903. In the lognormal case, the arithmetic mean income is derived as $\bar{y} = \exp\{\mu + \sigma^2/2\}$. Each aggregate revenue elasticity is obtained using a simulated population of 20,000 individuals, drawn at random from the distribution. As the results reported here assume that all incomes increase by the same proportion, the relative dispersion of incomes remains constant as incomes change over time.

Figure 7.4 shows aggregate elasticity profiles for income and all consumption taxes (for the non–proportional consumption case), and for total tax revenues, as incomes increase over a wide range of average income levels. The 20,000 values were selected randomly from an initial distribution with a lower mean of logarithms than that observed in the 2001 distribution. The average income increase, with a fixed variance of logarithms of income, was achieved by increasing all incomes by a fixed proportion each period. The non–equiproportional case involves a more complex process of income change, as shown below. This wide range either side of the 2001 average has been chosen to examine the sensitivity of the elasticities to extremes, even though revenue forecasts over such a long time period are most unlikely to be made on the assumption of fixed thresholds.

A strong feature of these profiles is that the elasticities are relatively stable, despite the wide range of average incomes considered, involving a

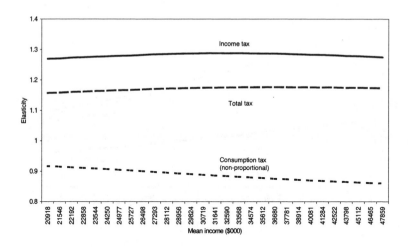

Figure 7.4: Aggregate Tax Revenue Elasticities

substantial movement of individuals from the lower income tax ranges to a situation in which a significant proportion of the income distribution faces the highest marginal income tax rate. For the highest average income shown, about one quarter of taxpayers are above the top threshold. The very slight tendency of the income tax elasticity to rise and then decline at higher average income levels is associated with this systematic upward movement of individuals through the thresholds as average income increases. The income and consumption tax elasticities are slightly below 1.3 and 0.9 respectively throughout the range. This result for the aggregate income tax revenue elasticity is consistent with the value obtained by Bell (2003), which uses a numerical approach with a very large sample of individual data from tax records, to which equi–proportional increases are applied.

Figure 7.5 shows how consumption tax elasticities depend on assumed saving behaviour. Revenue elasticity estimates are noticeably higher for the proportional consumption and 'no savings' cases (profiles A and B), but

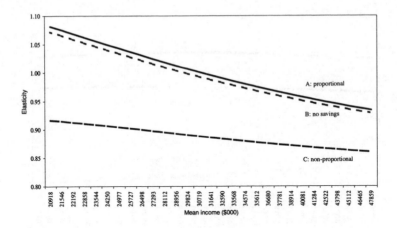

Figure 7.5: Aggregate Consumption Tax Revenue Elasticities

decline more rapidly as income rises, compared to the non–proportional case
in profile C. For example, at mean income levels of around NZ$30,000, elas-
ticities of about 1.0 and slightly below 0.9 are obtained from profiles A and C
respectively. Figure 7.5 also suggests that the effect on the revenue elasticity
of ignoring savings is not substantial provided, when income increases, the
proportion of income consumed remains approximately constant.

7.2.2   Non–equiproportional Income Changes

This subsection relaxes the assumption of equiproportionate income changes,
used in the previous subsection and in the vast majority of studies. In line
with the present approach of using parametric specifications at a fairly high
level of aggregation, this subsection first presents a function to describe the
systematic variation in $\eta_{y_i,Y}$ with y_i, and then presents revised aggregate
elasticities based on estimates of this dynamic specification.

A convenient functional form for the variation in $\eta_{y_i,Y}$ with y_i, involving just one parameter, is:

$$\eta_{y_i,Y} = 1 - (1 - \beta)(\log y_i - \mu) \tag{7.11}$$

where μ is the mean of logarithms of income (the logarithm of geometric mean income). In the case of lognormal income distributions, this is also the median income. This means that if $\beta < 1$ and y_i is less than geometric mean income, the elasticity, $\eta_{y_i,Y}$, is greater than unity, and *vice versa*, so that (7.11) involves equalising changes. If $\beta > 1$, income changes are disequalising. This specification can thus be used to examine the sensitivity of aggregate revenue elasticity measures to variations in the standard assumption of $\eta_{y_i,Y} = 1$. For non–equiproportional changes, the aggregate revenue elasticity can now be less than 1; for example it is zero if the only incomes which increase are below a tax–free threshold and none crosses the threshold.

In examining changes in total income arising from non–equiproportionate changes, according to equation (7.11), it is also useful, when increasing the 20,000 simulated incomes from one period to the next, to impose random proportionate income changes, in addition to the systematic equalising or disequalising tendency reflected in β. Without such changes, income inequality changes too rapidly to represent plausible annual changes. The specification in (7.11) is consistent with the following dynamic process, discussed in chapter 2. Let y_{it} denote individual i's income in period t, and let μ_t denote the mean of logarithms in period t, with $g_t = \exp(\mu_t)$ as the geometric mean. The generating process can be written as:

$$y_{i2} = \left(\frac{y_{i1}}{g_1}\right)^\beta \exp(\mu_2 + u_i) \tag{7.12}$$

where u_i is $N(0, \sigma_u^2)$. Equation (7.12) can be rewritten as:

$$(\log y_{i2} - \mu_2) = \beta(\log y_{i1} - \mu_1) + u_i \tag{7.13}$$

Hence the variance of logarithms of income in period 2, σ_2^2, is given by

$$\sigma_2^2 = \beta^2 \sigma_1^2 + \sigma_u^2 \tag{7.14}$$

The variance of logarithms is therefore constant when $\sigma_u^2 = \sigma_1^2 \left(1 - \beta^2\right)$.

Estimation of equation (7.13) was carried out for a range of pairs of consecutive years during the 1990s, using information from large samples of IR5 and IR3 filers. The results suggest a relatively stable value of β of around 0.85. This reflects a substantial degree of regression towards the (geometric) mean; indeed, with no random component of income change this would have the effect of halving income inequality in as little as three years. The degree of regression is expected to be lower for separate cohorts or age groups. Part of the overall regression reported here arises from the systematic component of change associated with age–earnings profiles. If $\beta = 0.85$ is combined with $\sigma_u^2 = 0.194$, the variance of logarithms of income remains constant over time. This value is in fact similar to that estimated for IR3 filers, though the values obtained for IR5 filers were lower, at about 0.1. Given that these samples do not constitute all taxpayers, and in practice inequality is relatively stable, it is probably appropriate here to model a stable variance of logarithms.

These values produce an aggregate income tax revenue elasticity, at 2001 mean income, of about 1.11. For the proportional and non–proportional consumption functions respectively, the aggregate consumption tax revenue elasticities are 0.93 and 0.83, giving corresponding total tax revenue elasticities of 1.05 and 1.03 respectively. Again, using a purely numerical approach to income tax elasticities, using a large sample of longitudinal income data, Bell (2003) found a very similar income tax revenue elasticity.

Regression towards the geometric mean therefore reduces the aggregate revenue elasticities. This arises because, for those above the geometric mean income, the value of $\eta_{T_{y,y_i}} \eta_{y_i,Y}$ is reduced, and *vice versa* for those below the geometric mean. The aggregate elasticity is a tax–share weighted average of these terms, and in view of the fact that T_{y_i}/T_Y increases as y increases, the lower values of $\eta_{T_y, y_i} \eta_{y_i, Y}$ at the upper income levels dominate.

To give some idea of the sensitivity of results to the variation in β, consider a value of $\beta = 0.9$, which requires $\sigma_u^2 = 0.133$ for a stable degree of income inequality. The aggregate income tax elasticity, again at 2001 mean income, is now 1.17, while the consumption tax elasticities are 0.96 and 0.85 for proportional and non–proportional consumption functions (giving total revenue elasticities of 1.11 and 1.07).

7.3 Conclusions

This chapter has examined the revenue responsiveness properties of New Zealand income and consumption taxes, based on the 2001 tax structure and expenditure patterns. Using the analytical expressions for revenue elasticities at the individual and aggregate levels, described earlier in this book, together with a simulated income distribution, values for New Zealand were obtained. Treating income growth as equiproportionate, these suggest that the aggregate income and consumption tax revenue elasticities are both fairly constant as mean income increases, at around 1.3 and 1.0 respectively. This latter estimate assumes that increases in disposable income are accompanied by approximately proportional increases in total expenditure. Allowing for non–equiproportionate income growth reduces revenue elasticities to around 1.1 (income tax) and 0.93 (consumption taxes). If there is a tendency for the savings proportion to increase as disposable income increases, a somewhat lower total consumption tax revenue elasticity, of around 0.85–0.90, is obtained at mean income levels approximating current levels in New Zealand. Examination of the tax–share weighted expenditure elasticities for various goods also revealed that, despite the adoption of a broad–based GST at a uniform rate in New Zealand, the persistence of various excises has an important effect on the overall consumption tax revenue elasticity, especially for individuals at relatively low income levels.

Appendix 7.1: Further Details of Elasticity Computations

Expenditure Elasticities

Expenditure elasticities were obtained using the published summary table of average expenditures over a range of income groups in the 2001 NZ House-hold Economic Survey (HES). This table divides all households in the sample into $K = 11$ income groups. Within each group the budget shares for each of $n = 58$ commodity groups were obtained by dividing average expenditure in each category by average total expenditure. Several commodity groups were excluded on the grounds that they more closely represented savings rather than expenditure. The ratio of averages is of course not the same as the average budget share (though earlier experiments using data for individual households showed that the differences were minor). Denote the arithmetic mean total expenditure of the kth group by m_k $(k = 1, ..., K)$ and the bud-get share of the ith commodity group and kth total expenditure group by w_{ki} $(i = 1, ..., n)$.

The raw values of these budget shares cannot be used to obtain elasticities because sampling variations, particularly for low–income and high– income groups, give rise to negative elasticities. Regressions were carried out of the form:

$$w_{ki} = a_{ik} + b_{ik} \log (m_k) + \frac{c_{ik}}{m_k} \qquad (7.15)$$

for each commodity group, i. In addition to providing a good fit in general, this specification has the advantage that weights based on the estimated parameters add to unity. However, it does not guarantee that the predicted weights always lie in the range $0 < w < 1$, though in practice this was not a serious problem; a few negative values at low total expenditure levels for some goods were set to zero and the other shares were adjusted accordingly to maintain the adding–up requirement. The smoothed budget shares were then used to calculate the total expenditure elasticities.

Differentiating (7.15), and dropping the k subscript, gives:

$$\frac{dw_i}{dm} = \frac{b_i y - c_i}{m^2} \qquad (7.16)$$

so that w_i unequivocally falls as m rises if $b_i < 0$ and $c_i > 0$; or if $c_i < 0$, so long as $m > c_i/b_i$. Alternatively, the share rises as income rises (that is, the income elasticity exceeds 1) if $b_i > 0$ and $c_i < 0$; or if $c_i > 0$, so long as $m > c_i/b_i$.

The coefficient estimates are reported in Tables 7.2 and 7.3. The required expenditure elasticities were obtained using:

$$e_{ki} = 1 + \frac{dw_{ki}}{dm_k} \frac{m_k}{w_{ki}} \qquad (7.17)$$

with dw/dm taken from differentiation of (7.15).

Income Distribution

The grouped frequency distribution of taxable income in New Zealand for 2000–2001 is given in Table 7.4. This distribution is for income from all sources, and covers employed and self employed individuals 15 years and older. A histogram of this distribution is shown in Figure 7.6, where a second mode right at the bottom of the distribution (below \$2000 per year) is evident. These very low annual incomes are likely to be associated with part time casual work by teenagers, or small amounts of interest income accruing to non–beneficiaries. Their (tax–share) contribution to the aggregate revenue elasticity is obviously negligible and there is nothing to be gained by modelling this mode in the present context. For this reason, the pragmatic solution was adopted of adjusting the frequencies in the bottom two groups of the distribution, as shown by smaller marked blocks for those income classes. Such bimodal distributions can in fact be modelled using a mixture distribution comprising a weighted average of lognormal and exponential distributions; see Bakker and Creedy (1999).

Table 7.2: Budget Share Regressions

	a	b	c	R^2
Fruit	-0.00829	0.002749	2.087083	0.260
Vegetables	0.054475	-0.00579	-1.37903	0.795
Meat	0.225018	-0.02806	-13.3021	0.733
Poultry	0.052294	-0.00617	-3.62406	0.303
Fish	0.001745	0.000182	0.429412	0.195
Farm products, fats, oils	0.126825	-0.01520	-4.4229	0.869
Cereals, cereal products	0.135981	-0.01589	-5.7208	0.888
Sweet products, beverages	0.139186	-0.01627	-7.28867	0.713
Other foodstuffs	0.152218	-0.01774	-8.35408	0.381
Meals away from home	-0.16374	0.03029	4.718327	0.971
Rent	0.622274	-0.08312	-1.83007	0.929
Payments to local authorities	-0.0882	0.013836	15.20095	0.950
Property maintenance goods	0.081228	-0.0069	-8.63439	0.718
Property maintenance	-0.68323	0.100973	43.35151	0.787
Housing expenses n.e.c.	-0.03517	0.004634	3.377435	0.742
Domestic fuel and power	0.196174	-0.02413	-0.94521	0.977
Home appliances	-0.00112	0.003079	2.134009	0.024
Household equipment	-0.00563	0.001527	0.727346	0.041
Furniture	-0.10488	0.017014	6.453542	0.741
Furnishings	-0.00076	0.000831	-0.64299	0.452
Floor coverings	-0.06074	0.008517	4.952152	0.462
Household textiles	-0.01107	0.002411	0.852601	0.125
Household supplies	0.078421	-0.00923	-4.4682	0.503
Household services	-0.08467	0.015257	16.66589	0.920
Men's clothing	-0.0772	0.01134	5.588882	0.523
Women's clothing	-0.17633	0.025524	13.84376	0.742
Children's clothing	-0.00054	0.000862	0.267848	0.027
Other Clothing	0.029442	-0.00308	-3.3534	0.868
Clothing supplies & services	-0.00295	0.000601	0.434927	0.015
Men's footwear	-0.02062	0.003132	1.23944	0.597
Women's footwear	-0.06346	0.008629	5.976196	0.878
Children's footwear	0.002005	-8.35E-05	-0.35364	0.250
Other Footwear	0.010164	-1.05E-03	-1.32814	0.780
Footwear supplies & services	0.003267	-3.81E-04	-0.3558	0.338
Public transport within NZ	-0.06172	0.009624	5.100902	0.503

Table 7.3: Budget Share Regressions (Continued)

	a	b	c	R^2
Overseas travel	-0.47099	0.07091	28.55522	0.788
Road vehicles	0.291782	-0.02883	-31.0849	0.653
Vehicle ownership expenses	0.625611	-0.0743	-42.9299	0.570
Private transport costs n.e.c	-0.01354	0.002442	1.589636	0.059
Tobacco products	0.166991	-0.0214	-8.79842	0.621
Alcohol	-0.12924	0.021882	7.49086	0.629
Medical goods	-0.02832	0.004974	3.036628	0.106
Toiletries and cosmetics	0.00956	0.000191	-0.92042	0.395
Personal goods	0.032463	-0.00257	-3.42718	0.589
Pets, racehorses and livestock	0.120291	-0.01498	-7.75913	0.470
Stationery and office equip	0.070482	-0.00593	-5.10796	0.308
Leisure goods	0.019047	0.000662	-4.02311	0.758
Recreational vehicles	0.011469	-0.00076	-2.11383	0.635
Goods n.e.c.	-0.01190	0.002321	0.9711	0.141
Health services	-0.12371	0.020146	11.10986	0.545
Personal services	-0.10878	0.015507	9.209476	0.353
Educational and tuition	0.026106	-0.00101	1.068944	0.175
Accommodation services	-0.07752	0.011855	4.266511	0.679
Fin, insurance and legal	0.097855	-0.00857	-2.83561	0.185
Vocational services	-0.00239	0.000818	-0.75566	0.897
Leisure services	-0.03519	0.009307	0.15564	0.865
Services n.e.c.	0.061889	-0.00639	-7.72831	0.461
Outgoings n.e.c.	0.207629	-0.02421	-17.3681	0.079

Table 7.4: Grouped Distribution of Taxable Income

Range (000s)	no.	Average Income	Range (000s)	no.	Average Income
–1	93,213	409.83	30–31	41,890	30,414.00
1–2	61,912	1,452.57	31–32	34,770	31,507.18
2–3	41,329	2,521.56	32–33	44,251	32,477.18
3–4	44,486	3,544.49	33–34	38,084	33,533.93
4–5	36,385	4,552.98	34–35	33,849	34,534.91
5–6	43,644	5,437.80	35–36	30,837	35,526.43
6–7	32,442	6,580.17	36–37	27,936	36,512.18
7–8	55,677	7,495.72	37–38	34,878	37,548.02
8–9	67,115	8,371.65	38–39	31,082	38,498.93
9– 9.5	66,408	9,267.31	39–40	25,273	39,483.37
9.5–10	42,052	9,707.22	40–41	27,987	40,563.92
10–11	143,426	10,669.95	41–42	30,355	41,480.31
11–12	89,621	11,513.70	42–43	17,037	42,551.03
12–13	74,977	12,571.58	43–44	19,855	43,478.16
13–14	80,137	13,429.31	44–45	20,373	44,647.87
14–15	163,260	14,396.08	45–46	15,506	45,453.50
15–16	53,649	15,422.00	46–47	15,027	46,560.53
16–17	52,664	16,568.82	47–48	15,720	47,510.66
17–18	38,984	17,472.11	48–49	17,132	48,471.26
18–19	48,558	18,469.33	49–50	12,519	49,700.59
19–20	46,773	19,566.15	50–52	28,862	51,011.51
20–21	47,134	20,556.02	52–54	26,642	52,891.96
21–22	37,598	21,524.06	54–56	19,947	54,980.98
22–23	37,181	22,572.31	56–58	24,379	56,876.89
23–24	35,388	23,539.56	58–60	19,203	59,208.08
24–25	32,699	24,518.45	60–65	52,194	62,407.42
25–26	31,564	25,449.60	65–70	24,748	67,319.34
26–27	30,796	26,333.18	70–80	43,913	74,481.48
27–28	37,842	27,465.45	80–90	22,783	85,128.34
28–29	35,810	28,586.43	90–100	19,963	94,708.39
29–30	35,872	29,622.28	> 100	47,218	182,074.25

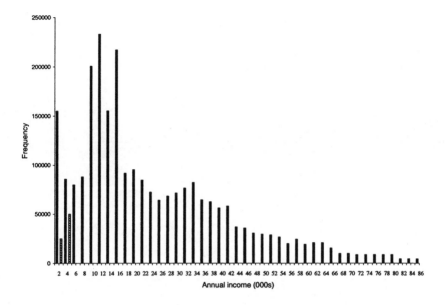

Figure 7.6: Income Distribution

The resulting distribution can then be modelled using a unimodal lognormal distribution, as discussed above, whose two parameters can be obtained directly as sample values of the mean and variance of logarithms. Further support for the lognormal is provided by the fact that the implied arithmetic mean value, using the properties of the lognormal mentioned earlier, was found to be close to the arithmetic mean calculated directly from the distribution.

Part IV

Conclusions

Chapter 8

Conclusions

In the analysis of taxation, economists are often occupied with welfare questions, concerning for example who gains and who loses from particular tax policies, or the nature of the optimal tax structure to maximise a social welfare function. Budgetary authorities, on the other hand, whilst not unconcerned about welfare issues, are often more focused on revenue aspects of the tax system, since these directly affect public spending plans. In this context, questions concern such issues as the way in which tax revenues respond to changes in tax rates, the effect on future tax revenues of income growth, whether discretionary changes to tax structures are likely to be required to ensure sufficient tax revenues, or the way in which tax changes affect the government's ability to redistribute income.

Despite the availability of a number of analytical tools to help policy advisers answer these questions, the revenue and distributional aspects of taxes have often been analysed in practice using fairly *ad hoc* or numerical–intensive approaches. However, in recent years the scope and sophistication of analytical tools available to explore tax revenue questions has increased. This book has focused on a particular revenue–related phenomenon, the built–in flexibility or revenue responsiveness of taxes, and has sought to summarise, synthesise and extend the principal methods currently available to facilitate such analyses. A key objective has been to consider tools which can readily

185

be applied in practice to data that are typically available for most tax systems, and to demonstrate how these can be applied to observed income and consumption tax structures.

8.1 Conceptual Issues

Part II concentrated on setting out a unified analytical framework within which the revenue responsiveness of income and consumption taxes could be assessed. Chapters 2 and 3 showed that tractable analytical expressions can be produced for the revenue responsiveness of income taxes, various indirect taxes and for combined direct–plus–indirect taxes, where the indirect tax system is combined with a general multi–step income tax structure. The principal measure highlighted was the tax revenue elasticity: the percentage change in tax revenue in association with a given percentage change in income, for a constant tax structure or structures. The results clarified the determinants of the revenue responsiveness properties of different taxes, and demonstrated that both income and consumption tax elasticities can be estimated from information that is generally available for most tax systems. This involved summary tax parameters and total expenditure elasticities for groups of taxed and untaxed commodities. Suitable income distribution data are also a prerequisite for any analysis of revenue elasticities in aggregate.

On income taxation, chapter 2 showed that the magnitude of revenue elasticities can be expected to differ substantially for alternative forms of income tax, and for the same tax over time as, for example, incomes change relative to tax thresholds. Chapter 3, on consumption taxation, showed that the income tax regime and individuals' savings behaviour are important determinants of the revenue elasticity of consumption taxes. The consumption tax structure is also important, involving a mixture of *ad valorem* taxes and excises, and the number and range of tax rates. In a uniform consumption tax rate system, consumption tax revenue must be income–inelastic provided the income tax system is progressive. However, the elasticity of total income–plus–consumption taxes must exceed unity.

For the more common two–rate or multi–rate cases, whether or not consumption tax revenue is elastic is ambiguous but depends on two simple conditions. These concern whether the income tax is regressive or progressive, and the average expenditure elasticity of zero–rated goods. Consumption taxes are more likely to be elastic if income taxes are regressive and if zero–rated goods are mainly necessities. In practice, while the latter condition often holds, the former does not, so that consumption taxes are expected typically to display inelastic revenue properties.

The revenue elasticity measures in chapters 2 and 3 are essentially statistical in nature, but chapter 4 showed how behavioural responses to the income tax system, in the form of labour supply effects, can be incorporated into revenue elasticity expressions. The primary objective was to identify how far, and in what circumstances, labour supply effects are quantitatively important for revenue responsiveness estimates, both for individual taxpayers and in aggregate. For individuals, this showed that even a relatively simple tax–benefit structure can produce labour supply responses which considerably alter tax revenue elasticity calculations. In aggregate the effects may not be large. However, this depends on individuals' attitudes towards working versus leisure and, for particular types of individual or household (such as female second–earners, pension recipients, and low–wage men), empirical estimation of revenue elasticities may have to be aware of the differential impact of wage growth.

The various tax parameters in the elasticity expressions obtained in Part II also highlight the potential impact of tax reform on built–in flexibility. When governments make discretionary changes to tax parameters, such as tax rates and allowances, the direct effect on tax revenue is of immediate concern both to the treasury and to taxpayers. These year–to–year changes generally have small impacts on revenue elasticities, but they can build up to more substantial effects over longer periods, especially when compounded by subsequent reforms. For example, from the early 1980s, many industrialised countries undertook significant tax reforms, often involving shifts towards less progressive income taxes and greater use of indirect taxes, as well as experiencing rising mean incomes relative to tax thresholds.

Results in Part II suggest that each of these changes can be expected to affect tax revenue elasticities, while commonly observed increases in the inequality of pre–tax incomes could also be important. Surprisingly, few attempts have been made to explore these issues empirically. Exceptions are the studies of income tax revenue elasticities for the UK and the US in the early 1980s identified in chapter 2, including Hutton and Lambert (1980), Fries *et al.* (1982) and Creedy and Gemmell (1982). For this reason, Part III presented three case studies, for the tax systems of Australia, New Zealand and the United Kingdom, which illustrate how the analytical tools in Part II can be applied in practice.

8.2   Revenue Elasticity Estimates

Part III began by looking at the revenue responsiveness properties of the UK's income and consumption taxes, calculating annual revenue elasticities since the late 1980s using annual Inland Revenue data on income tax allowances and deductions, and the personal income distribution. The results revealed that a component of the income tax revenue elasticity – the income elasticity of income–related deductions – was both quantitatively important and variable over time. It fell substantially with the limitation and then the withdrawal of mortgage interest tax relief, stabilised in the mid–1990s, and increased again in recent years with the rise in private pension schemes.

Income tax revenue elasticity estimates of around 1.2 in the early 1990s rose to around 1.4 by 2000. This rise appears to be partly in response to the increased pension deductions referred to above, and also to the reversal of some of the 1980s tax reforms as a more progressive structure was re–introduced. Estimates of elasticities for consumption taxes reveal that allowing for the impacts on the consumption tax revenue elasticity of the income tax system, savings and transfers is important. When these are included, values for the revenue elasticity around 0.7 are obtained for recent years, whereas when they are ignored, elasticity values appear to be around unity.

Chapter 6 turned to a different but related question: the extent to which redistribution can be achieved using a structure of consumption taxes with differential rates and exemptions. This showed that the revenue elasticity measure, typically used for revenue growth measurement, also provides a measure of the progressivity of the tax schedule at different income levels – liability progression. Focusing on consumption taxes, chapter 6 demonstrated that, unlike income taxes where different tax rates/thresholds can be targeted at particular income levels, different consumption tax rates provide a more limited redistributive devise. This primarily arises because most commodity groups (given a broad classification) are consumed to some degree by all households whatever their income, and the consumption tax equivalent of income tax thresholds – the extent to which spending is on taxed/untaxed goods – can only be influenced indirectly by policy changes. For example, changes in the classification of tax–exempt goods are likely to stimulate compensating changes in spending patterns, as observed in the UK with the levying of VAT on insurance and domestic fuel.

Thus although redistribution can be achieved by taxing most heavily those goods for which the income elasticity exceeds unity (for which the budget shares increase as income increases), there are strong limitations on the extent of redistribution possible, compared with, for example, what is achievable using income taxes. Progressivity was found to be maximised when only one commodity group, that having the largest total expenditure elasticity, is taxed. Where further commodity groups need to be taxed to meet revenue requirements, the tax rate should fall as the total expenditure elasticity falls. With a uniform structure, where some goods are exempt from a consumption tax, the liability progression is independent of the level of the tax rate.

Chapter 6 examined the Australian indirect tax structure, comparing it with alternative forms involving the taxation of only those groups for which the expenditure elasticity exceeds unity at all total expenditure levels. Using Australian Household Expenditure Survey data, it was found that even extreme forms of differentiation in indirect taxes have a relatively small effect on liability progression and inequality, confirming that consumption taxes provide only a blunt redistributive instrument.

Chapter 7, on New Zealand, returned to the measurement of revenue responsiveness for income and consumption taxes, examined in the UK context in chapter 5. However, in the New Zealand case, rather than calculate revenue elasticities retrospectively, profiles of revenue elasticities were reported for a variety of income and expenditure levels, using the 2001 tax structure and expenditure patterns. The New Zealand case is interesting because the income tax structure involves no initial tax–free allowance, and four steps with marginal rates ranging from 15 to 39 per cent. The consumption tax structure is also quite simple with a uniform–rate Goods and Services Tax (GST) with few exemptions, plus a small number of excise taxes. Treating income growth as equiproportionate, this structure yielded aggregate income and consumption tax revenue elasticities which were both fairly constant as mean income increases, at around 1.3 and 1.0 respectively.

Chapter 7 suggested a mechanism to allow for the non–equiproportionate income growth often observed in practice. This was found to reduce revenue elasticities to around 1.1 (income tax) and 0.93 (consumption taxes), at income levels approximating those current in New Zealand. The evidence also suggested that, despite the adoption of a broad–based GST at a uniform rate in New Zealand, the persistence of various excises has a noticeable effect on

Table 8.1: Comparing Aggregate Revenue Elasticities

Country	Year/ Regime	Income Tax	Consumption Tax
UK	1990	1.2	0.85
	2000	1.4	0.71
Australia	Pre–GST	1.5	0.82
	Post–GST	1.5	0.81
New Zealand	2001	1.1	0.93

the overall consumption tax revenue elasticity, especially for individuals at relatively low income levels.

It is interesting to compare the revenue elasticity estimates obtained for the three countries examined in Part III. Each country uses a multi–step income tax function with three or four steps but where the relevant thresholds occur at quite different points in the income scale. For example New Zealand, unlike Australia and the UK, has no initial tax–free threshold, while the higher income tax rates in Australia apply to individuals with lower (relative to mean) incomes than is the case in New Zealand or the UK. The three countries also now use a broad–based *ad valorem* sales/value added tax with a few exemptions (such as food in Australia and the UK, and rent in New Zealand), together with a set of excises, most notably on motor fuel, alcohol and tobacco.

Revenue elasticity estimates are summarised in Table 8.1. The income tax elasticities for Australia were obtained using the mid–1990s income tax structure, and relate to elasticities for mean incomes in that period, around A\$30,000 (see chapter 3). The same income tax structure and income levels are used to compare pre– and post–GST consumption tax revenue elasticities, though GST was not introduced until 2000. The country ranking of income tax elasticities accords with what might be expected given the progressivity of the respective income tax systems. The Australian income tax, with its high marginal rates at relatively low incomes reveals the highest elasticity, while the relatively flat New Zealand system, with lower top rates and no zero–rate band, has the lowest elasticity. As mentioned earlier, the increase in elasticity values for the intermediate country, the UK, also accords with expectations based on the increased progressivity of the UK income tax structure achieved in the late 1990s.

For consumption taxes, earlier chapters have shown that it is quite difficult for typical indirect tax systems to generate a revenue elasticity in excess of unity. It requires especially high tax rates on goods consumed predominantly by those on high incomes, in addition to income tax structures and savings habits which do not counteract this. Broad–based *ad valorem* taxes with one or two rates are not generally capable of achieving an elastic outcome. In addition, it is common for alcohol, tobacco and/or motor fuel to be amongst the most heavily taxed goods, spending on which is not typically dominated by high income households.

Table 8.1 confirms that consumption tax revenue elasticities are consistently less than unity in all three countries. As with income taxes, however, the system with the least progressive income tax and most uniform set of indirect tax rates – New Zealand – has an elasticity value closest to unity. Consumption tax revenue elasticities appear especially low in the UK in recent years. As chapter 5 showed, this partly reflects the rising progressivity of income taxes in the UK, but is substantially due to the shift in consumption patterns during the 1991–95 period, towards those items with relatively low tax–share weighted expenditure elasticities. In Australia, the elasticity of the pre– and post–GST systems appears very similar despite the numerous changes to tax rates. This largely reflects the fact that the distribution of pre– and post–GST effective tax rates across commodity groups is similar; the correlation between pre– and post–GST effective (tax–inclusive) tax rates for the 14 commodity groups in Table 6.2 is 0.97.

8.3 Elasticities and Redistribution

Since revenue elasticities of taxes also measure liability progression it is tempting to draw inferences regarding progressivity and redistribution from elasticity estimates. However, it should be remembered that the aggregate revenue elasticity, whether for a specified tax or combined tax system, provides only a crude measure of the overall progressivity of the tax *structure*. Such elasticities do not identify whether the tax or tax system is progressive at all income or expenditure levels. Hence chapter 6 examined liability progression for Australian consumption taxes across a wide range of household expenditure levels.

This revealed interesting examples of both ambiguous and unambiguous tax structures with respect to progressivity. The pre–GST system appeared to be characterised by elastic values below expenditures of about $500 per week, and inelastic above $500. The progressivity of the tax structure was therefore ambiguous, *ceteris paribus* generating redistribution toward those with expenditures around $500 and away from those above or below this level; that is, it was progressive below, but regressive above, $500. The post–GST system, however, appeared to be elastic at all expenditure levels, and declining monotonically as expenditure increased, suggesting an unambiguously progressive structure, despite being less progressive at low expenditure levels than the pre–GST system.

Notwithstanding this evidence, neither aggregate nor individual revenue elasticities can be used to comment directly on overall redistribution or inequality since they take no account of either the numbers of individuals facing different tax rates, or the appropriate welfare weighting of different individuals or households. Conclusions regarding redistribution drawn from evidence on elasticities should therefore be interpreted carefully. For this reason, chapter 6, which dealt explicitly with inequality issues, reported additional measures of inequality and social welfare. However, these measures are typically derived under more or less restrictive assumptions, so that outcomes must be recognised as conditional on the validity of these assumptions, such as the exclusion of complements by using additive utility functions.

Nevertheless, governments are often interested in whether their tax systems are likely to foster or discourage a redistribution of incomes across individuals or households with different gross incomes. For this more limited exercise, individual revenue elasticities, estimated across income or expenditure levels, provide a useful summary statistic. They may be used to help identify those income or expenditure ranges, or types of individual or household, from whom a specified tax takes proportionately more income. How this is redistributed depends, among other things, on the incidence of the resulting public expenditure.

8.4   Implications for Policy

Any analysis of taxation is, by its nature, potentially relevant for policy. This book has concentrated on revenue growth aspects of taxes which, because they often relate to the longer term, may be undervalued in the heat of short–term policy debates. However, there are several relevant conclusions for policy–makers to be drawn from the analyses in previous chapters.

Firstly, precisely because the implications of tax policy changes for revenue growth may not be quantitatively important for a number of years, it is tempting to ignore them. However, some discretionary tax changes which raise tax revenues immediately may reduce the future growth of revenues, while other discretionary changes may raise immediate revenues, along with their future growth. Under–indexing of personal income tax allowances, so that real allowances fall, can be an example of the former. Raising the top marginal income tax rate can be an example of the latter policy. It is important for policy–makers to appreciate the distinction between these two types of tax policy.

Secondly, in setting tax parameters, it is easy for policy–makers to focus on each tax within a system separately. However, as the analysis of consumption tax revenue elasticities demonstrates, decisions affecting income tax revenues can have important consequences for indirect tax revenue growth. Thus, unintended effects on revenue growth may readily arise from policy changes intended to achieve some more immediate outcome. The rising progressivity of income taxes in the UK since the mid–1990s provides a possible example. This has raised the long–run revenue growth prospects for income taxes, which may or may not have been intended or anticipated. But it has also served to reduce future consumption tax revenue growth which was probably not intended.

Thirdly, redistributional policies more generally have been shown in previous chapters to have revenue consequences, and *vice versa*. Thus, within the same tax, there may be unintended effects on redistribution arising from tax policy decisions designed to affect revenues. Similar outcomes can arise across taxes where the interactions between taxes transmit the impacts of policy changes in one tax onto another. The effects on indirect tax revenues from changes to income tax progressivity is a common example.

Fourthly, behavioural responses to some tax policy changes may be quantitatively important for revenue growth. Chapter 5 highlighted the case of the tax–deductibility of pension contributions in the UK. Such policies are often initiated to encourage private savings and ease the future public financing burden of an ageing population. To the extent that this achieves the desired behavioural response, one consequence of this, almost certainly unforeseen or at least unquantified, is that the elasticity of income tax deductions increases. This tends to suppress future income tax revenue growth. The immediate, direct reduction in income tax revenues is, of course, more readily quantifiable.

The impact of behavioural responses in the form of labour supply changes associated with wage growth was the focus of chapter 4. Though conventional labour supply estimates suggest the overall effects on income tax revenues are not large, recent literature on other behavioural responses to tax reform point to potentially much larger impacts. Thus Feldstein (1999) and Slemrod (2001), for example, have stressed the potential for substantial tax avoidance responses, when tax rates increase, via shifts towards untaxed forms of compensation, or types of expenditure attracting lower tax rates. As real wage rates rise with a given tax structure, real fiscal drag can be expected to push increasing numbers into higher income tax brackets, in the absence of increased avoidance behaviour. However, in these circumstances, individuals might be expected to respond, via labour supply changes or other tax avoidance measures, to seek to minimise taxable income at the margin, with direct revenue consequences.

Finally, this book has focused on personal income and consumption taxes. But the analytics of revenue growth are important for other major taxes such as social insurance contributions and taxes on corporate profits. Many social insurance schemes act analogously to a tax on personal incomes and hence their revenue responsiveness properties may be assessed using the same methods as those proposed for income taxes in previous chapters. In addition, where social insurance contributions are thought likely to affect consumption tax revenues, via reductions in disposable incomes, they may need to be incorporated into such responsiveness calculations. Estimating revenue elasticities for corporation taxes is likely to be a much more difficult exercise, in part because of the complexity of many corporate tax systems used in practice, and in part because of the nature and volatility of the tax base – company profits. Nevertheless, social insurance and corporate tax policies, designed to achieve short–run revenue, distributional or other objectives, have longer term revenue effects. Future research could therefore usefully develop the analytics for these cases.

Bibliography

[1] Aitchison, J.A. and Brown, J.A.C. (1957) *The Lognormal Distribution*. Cambridge: Cambridge University Press.

[2] Bakker, A. and Creedy, J. (1999) Macroeconomic variables and income inequality in New Zealand: an exploration using conditional mixture distributions. *New Zealand Economic Papers*, 33, pp. 59–79.

[3] Bell, M. (2003) Fiscal drag and the long term fiscal model. New Zealand Treasury internal paper.

[4] Bingley, P. and Lanot, G. (2002) The incidence of income tax on wages and labour supply. *Journal of Public Economics*, 83, pp. 173–194.

[5] Blackorby, C. and Donaldson, D. (1988) Money metric utility: a harmless normalization? *Journal of Economic Theory*, 46, pp. 120–129.

[6] Blundell, R. and MaCurdy, T. (1999) Labour supply: a survey of alternative approaches. In *Handbook of Labor Economics*, Vol. 3. (ed. by O. Ashenfelter and D. Card). Amsterdam: North–Holland.

[7] Blundell, R. and Walker, I. (1982) Modelling the joint determination of household labour supplies and commodity demands. *Economic Journal*, 92, pp. 351–364.

[8] Blundell, R., Duncan, A. and Maghir, C. (1998) Estimating labour supply responses using tax reforms. *Econometrica*, 66, pp. 827–861.

[9] Caminada, K. and Goudswaard, K. (1996) Progression and revenue effects of income tax reform. *International Tax and Public Finance*, 3, pp. 57–66.

[10] Carter, C. (1981) The income elasticity of the Georgia state income tax. *Federal Reserve Bank of Atlanta Economic Review*, 66, pp. 15–21.

[11] Chennels, L., Dilnot, A. and Roback, N. (2000) *A Survey of the UK Tax System.* London: Institute for Fiscal Studies.

[12] Chisholm, A., Freebairn, J. and Porter, M. (1990) A goods and services tax for Australia. *Australian Forum*, 7, pp. 127–190.

[13] Clarke, T., Dilnot, A., Goodman, A. and Myck, M. (2002) Taxes and transfers 1997–2001. *Oxford Review of Economic Policy*, 18, pp. 187–201.

[14] Creedy, J. (1985) *Dynamics of Income Distribution.* Oxford: Basil Blackwell.

[15] Creedy, J. (1992) Revenue and progressivity neutral changes in the tax mix. *Australian Economic Review*, 2, pp. 31–38.

[16] Creedy, J. (1996) *Fiscal Policy and Social Welfare: An Analysis of Alternative Tax and Transfer Systems.* Aldershot: Edward Elgar.

[17] Creedy, J. (1998) Are consumption taxes regressive? *Australian Economic Review*, 31, pp. 107–116.

[18] Creedy, J. (1999) Indirect tax reform in Australia: the welfare effects on different demographic groups. *Australian Economic Papers*, 38, pp. 367–392.

[19] Creedy, J. (2001) *Taxation and Economic Behaviour.* Cheltenham: Edward Elgar.

[20] Creedy, J. and Duncan, A. (2002) Behavioural microsimulation with labour supply responses. *Journal of Economic Surveys*, 16, pp. 1–39.

[21] Creedy, J. and Gemmell, N. (1982) The built–in flexibility of progressive income taxes: A simple model. *Public Finance*, 37, pp. 362–371.

[22] Creedy, J. and Gemmell, N. (1984) Income redistribution through taxes and transfers in Britain. *Scottish Journal of Political Economy*, 31, pp. 44–59.

[23] Creedy, J. and Gemmell, N. (1985) The indexation of taxes and transfers in Britain. *Manchester School*, 55, pp. 364–384.

[24] Creedy, J. and Gemmell, N. (2002a) The revenue responsiveness of consumption taxes. *Economic Record*, 78, pp. 186–194.

[25] Creedy, J. and Gemmell, N. (2002b) The built–in flexibility of income and consumption taxes: a survey. *Journal of Economic Surveys*, 14, pp. 509–532.

[26] Creedy, J. and Gemmell, N. (2003) The income elasticity of tax revenue for income and consumption taxes in the UK, *The Manchester School*, 71, pp. 641–658.

[27] Creedy, J. and Gemmell, N. (2004a) The revenue responsiveness of income and consumption taxes in the UK, *Fiscal Studies*, 25, pp. 55–77.

[28] Creedy, J. and Gemmell, N. (2004b) The built–in flexibility of income and consumption taxes in New Zealand. *Australian Economic Papers*, 43, pp. 459–474.

[29] Creedy, J. and Gemmell, N. (2005) Wage growth and income tax revenue elasticities with endogenous labour supply, *Economic Modelling*, 22, pp. 21–38.

[30] Deaton, A.S. and Muellbauer, J. (1980) *Economics and Consumer Behaviour*. Cambridge: Cambridge University Press.

[31] Delorme, C.C. and Hayakawa, H. (1977) The specification of the demand for money and the built–in flexibility of taxation in a multiplier–accelerator model. *Public Finance*, 32, pp. 48–54.

[32] Disney, R. and Smith S. (2002) The labour supply effect of the abolition of the earnings rule for older workers in the United Kingdom. *Economic Journal*, 112, pp. C136–C152.

[33] Dorrington, J.C. (1974) A structural approach to estimating the built–in flexibility of United Kingdom taxes on personal income. *Economic Journal*, 84, pp. 576–594.

[34] Dye, R.F. and McGuire, T.J. (1991) Growth and variability of state individual income and general sales taxes. *National Tax Journal*, 44, pp. 55–66.

[35] Feldstein, M. (1999) Tax avoidance and the deadweight loss of the income tax. *Review of Economics and Statistics*, 81, pp. 674–680.

[36] Fox, W.F. and Campbell, C. (1984) Stability of the state sales tax income elasticity. *National Tax Journal*, 37, pp. 201–212.

[37] Friedlaender, A.F., Swanson, G.J. and Due, J.F. (1973) Estimating sales tax revenue changes in response to changes in personal income and sales tax rates. *National Tax Journal*, 26, pp. 103–113.

[38] Fries, A., Hutton, J.P. and Lambert, P.J. (1982) The elasticity of the US individual income tax: its calculation, determinants and behavior. *Review of Economics and Statistics*, 64, pp. 147–151.

[39] Frisch, R. (1959) A complete system for computing all direct and cross demand elasticities in a model with many sectors. *Econometrica*, 27, pp. 177–196.

[40] Gemmell, N. (1985) Tax revenue shares and income growth: a note. *Public Finance*, 40, pp. 137–145.

[41] Giles, C. and Hall, J. (1998) Forecasting the PSBR outside government: the IFS perspective. *Fiscal Studies*, 19, pp. 83–100.

[42] Giorno, C., Richardson, P., Roseveare, D. and Van den Noord, P. (1995) Estimating potential output, output gaps and structural budget balances. *OECD Economics Department Working Papers*, no. 152.

[43] Greytak, D. and Thursby, J. (1979) Functional form in state income tax elasticity estimation. *National Tax Journal*, 32, pp. 195–200.

[44] Groves, H.M. and Kahn, H.C. (1952) The stability of state and local tax yields. *American Economic Review*, 52, pp. 87–102.

[45] Hart, P.E. (1975) Moment distributions in economics: an exposition. *Journal of the Royal Statistical Society, Series A*, 138, pp. 423–434.

[46] Heinemann, F. (2001) After the death of inflation: will fiscal drag survive? *Fiscal Studies*, 22, pp. 527–546.

[47] Hutton, J.P. (1980) Income tax elasticity and the distribution of income, with an application to Peninsular Malaysia. *South East Asia Economic Review*, 1, pp. 13–34.

[48] Hutton, J.P. and Lambert, P.J. (1980) Evaluating income tax revenue elasticities. *Economic Journal*, 90, pp. 901–906.

[49] Hutton, J.P. and Lambert, P.J. (1982a) Modelling the effects of income growth and discretionary change on the sensitivity of U.K. income tax revenue. *Economic Journal*, 92, pp. 145–155.

[50] Hutton, J.P. and Lambert, P.J. (1982b) Simulating the revenue elasticity of an individual income tax. *Economic Letters*, 9, pp. 175–179.

[51] Hutton, J.P. and Lambert, P.J. (1983) Inequality and revenue elasticity in tax reform. *Scottish Journal of Political Economy*, 30, pp. 221–234.

[52] Johnson, D. (1999) The impact of new tax legislation on households. *Family Matters*, 54, pp. 55–59.

[53] Johnson, D., Manning, I. and Hellwig, O. (1995) *Trends in The Distribution of Cash Income and Non–cash Benefits.* Canberra: Australian Government Printing Services.

[54] Johnson, D., Freebairn, J., Creedy, J., Scutella, R. and Cowling, S. (1997) *A Stocktake of Taxation in Australia.* Melbourne: Melbourne Institute of Applied Economic and Social Research.

[55] Johnson, D., Freebairn, J. and Scutella, R. (1999) *Evaluation of the Government's Tax Package.* Melbourne: Melbourne Institute of Applied Economic and Social Research.

[56] Johnson, P. and Lambert, P. (1989) Measuring the revenue responsiveness of income tax revenue to income growth: a review and some UK values. *Fiscal Studies*, 10, pp. 1–18.

[57] Kay, J.A. and Morris, C.N. (1979) Direct and indirect taxes: some effects of the 1979 Budget. *Fiscal Studies*, 1, pp. 1–10.

[58] King, M. A. (1983) Welfare analysis of tax reforms using household data. *Journal of Public Economics*, 21, pp. 183–214.

[59] Lambert, P.J. (1993) *The Distribution and Redistribution of Income: A Mathematical Analysis.* Manchester: Manchester University Press.

[60] Legler J.B. and Shapiro, P. (1968) The responsiveness of state tax revenue to economic growth. *National Tax Journal*, 21, pp. 46–56.

[61] Lluch, C., Powell, A. and Williams, R. (1977) *Patterns in Household Demand and Saving.* Oxford: Oxford University Press for the World Bank.

[62] Musgrave, R.A. and Thin, T. (1948) Income tax progression. *Journal of Political Economy*, 56, pp. 498–514.

[63] Özmucur, S. (1979) More on built–in flexibility of taxation. *Public Finance*, 34, pp. 443–451.

[64] Peel, D.A. (1979) On the built–in flexibility of taxation and the deterministic and the stochastic stability of macro–models under alternative expectations schemes. *Public Finance*, 34, pp. 258–266.

[65] Pike, T. and Savage, D. (1998) Forecasting the public finances in the Treasury. *Fiscal Studies*, 19, pp. 49–62.

[66] Podder, N. (1997) Tax elasticity, income redistribution and the measurement of tax progressivity. In *Research on Economic Inequality*, Vol. 7. (ed. by S. Zandvakili), pp. 39–60. Greenwich: JAI Press.

[67] Pohjola, M. (1985) Built–in flexibility of progressive taxation and the dynamics of income: stability, cycles, or chaos? *Public Finance* , 40, pp. 263–273.

[68] Ram, R. (1991) Elasticity of individual income tax in the United States: Further evidence from cross–section data. *National Tax Journal*, 44, pp. 93–99.

[69] Robinson, W. (1987) How buoyant is public revenue? *Fiscal Studies*, 8, pp. 35–47.

[70] Sah, R.K. (1983) How much redistribution is possible through indirect taxes. *Journal of Public Economics*, 12, pp. 83–102.

[71] Scutella, R. (1997) The incidence of indirect taxes on final demand in Australia. *Melbourne Institute of Applied Economic and Social Research Working Paper*, no. 18/97.

[72] Sentance, A., Hall, S. and O'Sullivan, J. (1998) Modelling and forecasting UK public finances. *Fiscal Studies*, 19, pp. 63–81.

[73] Singer, N.M. (1970) Estimating state income tax revenues: a new approach. *Review of Economics and Statistics*, 52, pp. 427–433.

[74] Slemrod, J. (2001) A general model of behavioural response to taxation, *International Tax and Public Finance*, 8, pp. 119–128.

[75] Smith, P.E. (1963) A note on the built–in flexibility of the individual income tax. *Econometrica*, 31, pp. 704–711.

[76] Smyth, D.J. (1974) Built–in flexibility of taxation and stability in a simple dynamic IS–LM model. *Public Finance*, 29, pp. 111–114.

[77] Smyth, D.J. (1978) Built–in flexibility of taxation, the government budget constraint, the specification of the demand for money function, and the stability of an IS–LM system. *Public Finance*, 33, pp. 367–375.

[78] Sobel, R.S. and Holcombe, R.G. (1996) Measuring the growth and variability of tax bases over the business cycle. *National Tax Journal*, 49, pp. 534–552.

[79] Sood, R. and Scutella, R. (1997) Description of the current Australian indirect tax system. *Melbourne Institute of Applied Economic and Social Research Working Paper*, no. 19/97.

[80] Spahn, P.B. (1975) Simulating long–term changes of income distribution within an income tax model for West Germany. *Public Finance*, 30, pp. 231–250.

[81] Stern, N. (1990) Uniformity versus selectivity in indirect taxation. *Economics and Politics*, 2, pp. 83–102.

[82] Suyderhoud, J.P. and Veseth, M. (1976) The effect of inflation on the income elasticity of taxes. *Public Finance Quarterly*, 4, pp. 323–337.

[83] Tanzi, V. (1969) Measuring the sensitivity of the Federal income tax from cross–section data: a new approach. *Review of Economics and Statistics*, 51, pp. 206–209.

[84] Tanzi, V. (1976) The sensitivity of the yield of the U.S. individual income tax and the tax reforms of the past decade. *IMF Staff Papers*, 23, pp. 441–454.

[85] van den Noord, P. (2000) The size and role of automatic fiscal stabilizers in the 1990s and beyond. *OECD Economics Department Working Paper*, no. 230.

[86] Vickrey, W. (1949) Some limits to the income elasticity of income tax yields. *Review of Economics and Statistics*, 31, pp. 140–144.

[87] Wasylenko, M. (1975) Estimating the elasticity of state personal income taxes. *National Tax Journal*, 28, pp. 139–142.

[88] Wilford, W.T. (1965) State tax stability criteria and the revenue–income coefficient reconsidered. *National Tax Journal*, 18, pp. 304–312.

[89] Young, L. (2002) *Ad valorem* indirect tax rates in New Zealand. New Zealand Treasury Internal Paper.

Index

abbreviated welfare functions 151–2

ad valorem tax rates 44–7, 138–41, 161–3, 164

ad valorem taxes 8

  see also Goods and Services Tax (GST) (Australia); Goods and Services Tax (GST) (New Zealand); Value Added Tax (VAT)

additive utility functions 149, 155, 156

after-income-tax income *see* disposable income

aggregate consumption tax revenue elasticities 58–9, 60, 63–6, 119, 169, 170–72

aggregate income 53, 107

aggregate income tax revenue elasticities

  calculation 36–8, 60

  and equiproportional income changes 22–3, 34, 107–8, 113, 169, 170–72

  general case 21–4, 34

  and income distribution 8, 21, 22–4, 108

  and labour supply 84–8

  multi-step income tax function 31–2, 34, 107–8

  non-equiproportional income changes 22, 23–4

  single-step tax function 33–4

  UK 110, 113–16

aggregate income tax revenues, UK 105–6

aggregate revenue elasticities

  calculation 84–8

  and equiproportional income changes 169–72

  and income distribution 8, 11, 37–8, 60, 170–75, 177, 180–81

  information 60, 169–70

  New Zealand 169–75, 176–81

  and non-equiproportional income changes 172–5

  non-technical summary 11

  regression analyses 5–6

  simulation models 5